a private life

MICHAEL KIRBY

a private life

fragments, memories, friends

ALLEN&UNWIN

Published by Allen & Unwin in 2011

Allen & Unwin
Sydney, Melbourne, Auckland, London

83 Alexander Street
Crows Nest NSW 2065
Australia
Phone: (61 2) 8425 0100
Fax: (61 2) 9906 2218
Email: info@allenandunwin.com
Web: www.allenandunwin.com

Cataloguing-in-Publication details are available
from the National Library of Australia
www.trove.nla.gov.au

ISBN 978 1 74237 620 2

Text design by Brittany Britten
Set in 11.5/15 pt Granjon by Bookhouse, Sydney
Printed and bound in Australia by Griffin Press

10 9 8 7 6 5 4 3

To my father, Don Kirby

contents

INTRODUCTION *ix*

1. OF FRECKLES, CROWNS AND CANES—
MY EARLY TEACHERS *1*

2. AFTER WOLFENDEN—HOW SCIENCE AND
LAW CAME TO THE RESCUE *25*

3. MY FRIEND JIMMY DEAN—
A NOSTALGIC JOURNEY *43*

4. JOHAN—LESSONS IN LOVE *65*

5. RIVERVIEW—
A MODERN MORALITY TALE *95*

6. OUT IN AFRICA—
OF JUDGES, AIDS AND TRUTH *115*

7. THE SALVOS—
A SURPRISING VISIT TO THE CITADEL *149*

8. THE PRINCE—IN DANGEROUS TIMES *167*

9. BUGGER THE ROSES—
REFLECTIONS ON RELATIVITIES *185*

BIBLIOGRAPHY *193*

INDEX *195*

INTRODUCTION

THIS IS NOT AN autobiography. There are too many gaps between the segments of my life described in the chapters. Moreover, it does not recount the story of my public life: as a practising lawyer, in university bodies, the Council for Civil Liberties, the Australian Law Reform Commission, the courts and international agencies. Those who thirst for such details can find more than enough to slake that thirst in the recent biography of me by A.J. Brown, *Michael Kirby: Paradoxes/Principles*. More details of my judicial work are found in the large doorstopper, *Appealing to the Future: Michael Kirby and his Legacy*, edited by Ian Freckelton SC and Hugh Selby.

Just when you were thinking you had enough to read about my life, now comes this book. Allen & Unwin, the publisher, was convinced that an untapped well of interest existed of readers keen to hear my own voice. And so these essays have been compiled to offer fragments of memory about vivid times in my life from my earliest school days to recent years.

Why would anyone be interested in the private life of someone who served on the nation's highest court, but has now retired? Time will tell whether they are. In my own mind, the only justifications I could see were to demonstrate the lessons taught to me at law school by my great teacher, Julius Stone. At a time when Chief Justice Sir Owen Dixon was proclaiming that judicial experience and values were, and should be, immaterial to case outcomes, Julius Stone was providing antidotes. He taught his students that judges and lawyers had to be very aware of the impact on their minds and values of their life's experiences. To pretend that law was wholly objective might be a comforting fiction to which many (particularly conservative) proponents of the vocation adhered. But it was not what actually happened. Judges of our legal tradition have discretions and 'leeways for choice', as Stone taught. The words of the Constitution are often obscure; the language of statutes is commonly ambiguous; and the reasoning of common law decisions is frequently opaque. Judges, and especially in the highest courts, have important responsibilities to give meaning to the law and to declare its content. In doing so, they cannot but be affected by their values and by their attitudes to legal policy, legal principles and even past legal authority.

In this sense, the revelation of elements of judicial lives may help citizens to understand the influences that may be apparent, as undercurrents, in the formal reasoning that judges give for their decisions. Why one judge favours an interpretation that upholds Aboriginal rights where others reject the proposition may become clearer by understanding the lives, experiences and values of the several judicial decision-makers. This book therefore offers a candid glimpse into some of the early, and recent, forces that have affected my life and the influences upon my approaches to the resolution of human problems, including where those problems are dressed up in the raiments of judicial decisions.

One set of values, evident in this book, is a distaste for irrational prejudice and discrimination. As several chapters disclose, I grew up in an Australia rather different from the nation as it is today. It was a land of White Australia, where the participation of citizens of different races was discouraged and even effectively forbidden by prohibiting migration of non-Caucasian people. This attitude informed the laws and practices of the nation from colonial times until finally abolished after 1966. It took many more decades to remove (or at least reduce) the attitudes of racial prejudice that flowed deep in the Australian psyche. Remnants of those attitudes survive in Australia to this day.

Likewise, the approach of distain and disrespect for the dignity and legal rights of Australia's indigenous peoples was evident in many aspects of the law, including in the refusal to recognise the land rights of Aboriginals and Torres Strait Islanders. That refusal endured until the important decision of the High Court of Australia in *Mabo v Queensland [No.2]*. Although that decision was made before my appointment to the High Court, its consequences were felt in decisions made throughout my service. They included the decision in *Wik Peoples v Queensland*, where my vote proved decisive in the High Court in extending the Mabo principle to the vast pastoral leases that occupy huge areas of the Australian continent. Native title and pastoral leases had to be reconciled.

Discrimination against, or disrespect for, women, prisoners, migrants and others arose in the study of the law affecting the outcomes of many cases in which I participated in the High Court. I would be less than honest if I did not acknowledge that my own experience, as a homosexual man, made me very sensitive to discrimination. If you have tasted irrational discrimination, you do not like it. And you do not want others needlessly to be on the receiving end.

Many of the chapters in this book recount my acquaintance with discrimination in the area of sexuality. The chapter on the Wolfenden reforms was initially written for *Meanjin*, the Melbourne University intellectual quarterly, and first published in 2007. It celebrated the fiftieth anniversary of the reforms to the criminal law on homosexuals in England. Those reforms were later to be copied throughout Australia. Yet the old laws remain in place in most of the countries that were once part of the British Empire.

My essay on James Dean, the movie actor, describes the loneliness that the cruel laws against gay people occasioned in the 1950s. It is a metaphor for the loneliness and alienation that derives from discriminatory laws and practices generally.

The chapter on my partner, Johan van Vloten, gives an insight into his intelligence and grace that have illuminated my life since we met on 11 February 1969. Anyone who would deny another human being such blessings is trapped in unkind or unthinking formalism. Whether one is gay or straight, discovering a life's companion is something that most hearts yearn for. It is good for one's mental and spiritual health. Other citizens who would deny full equality in legal rights (including on relationship recognition) need to examine the question: by what rational entitlement do they presume to do so?

There follow several chapters that describe particular events and people in my life in recent years, many of them connected with the global and national struggles against the human immunodeficiency virus (HIV) that causes the condition of acquired immune deficiency syndrome (AIDS). Without treatment and care, HIV is usually fatal for the human beings who are infected with it. By one of those ironies of history, because HIV first struck the gay community in several countries, it brought many in the frontline out into the open. This is what happened to Johan and me. In the context of the enormous epidemic, where friends were dying in large numbers, the artificial obligation not to ask and not to tell suddenly seemed by the 1980s, indecent, humiliating, unacceptable.

Here too are stories of a visit in 2001 to Riverview College in Sydney, a privileged school of the enlightened Jesuits. It was a visit that upset some adherents to the Roman Catholic Church that has described homosexual acts as a propensity to 'evil'. The visit was named as unacceptable by Senator Bill Heffernan, who later falsely attacked my reputation in the Senate of the Australian Parliament. My basic offence, it seems, was that I was not sufficiently ashamed of myself and of my sexuality. This was so, although science demonstrated its common manifestation as just one further variation of the human species. Well, shame was over so far as I was concerned.

My encounters with the Salvation Army in Sydney, with judges grappling with the HIV epidemic in Africa, and with a brave Indian prince who had come out follow. These are vignettes in a life of many attempts, some unavailing, to spread enlightenment and a greater kindness.

The opening and the closing chapters of this book are respectively about my early education in public schools in Australia and my life now as someone growing older. And hopefully wiser. The book reveals a community and a nation which has been on the journey to remove every unlovely vestige of discrimination against people on the ground of sexual orientation. We need to learn from these changes. And to apply what we learn to other groups and causes that matter: the rights of refugees; the enduring human dignity of prisoners; the rights of drug dependent people and others who use drugs; sex workers and transgender citizens; the entitlements of people living with disabilities; the special features of the lives of the young and of the old; and the need for greater respect for other sentient animals caught up in the industry of slaughter for food.

The struggle for civilisation is never finished. When I was aged nine, I received a copy of the *Universal Declaration of Human Rights*. It profoundly influenced my thinking and its influence endures. However, new insights arise. Globalism has meant that we now share these insights with our fellow humans everywhere on the internet, in social networks and global media. The chapters of this book will describe my journey through life. Everyone has similar experiences. These are just mine.

Michael Kirby
24 August 2011

OF FRECKLES, CROWNS AND CANES— MY EARLY TEACHERS

SHE WAS TALL AND spare. She was friendly enough but, underneath that sweet exterior, was a voice of cold command. It was not to be messed with. She needed that voice to keep control over the thirty or so boys and girls—five year olds—in her charge. She was Mrs Church: my first teacher. Her specialities were plasticine and the piano. Anything to keep our young minds occupied and out of mischief.

Like many members of my family, Mrs Church was a Celt. She wore the badge of that warrior people, as two of my siblings— Donald and Diana—were to do. Red hair. And freckles. Lots of freckles, right up her arms. 'Don't go out in the sun, Donald,' we would say. 'Or you'll get freckles like Mrs Church.' Donald's eyes would fill with unwept tears, making his pale unfreckled skin around his eyes redder than ever. Getting as many freckles as Mrs Church was definitely not the way to go.

The year was 1944 and Mrs Church ran a tiny kindergarten in the parish hall attached to St Andrew's Anglican Church. That church and hall still stand on the corner of Concord Road and Parramatta Road in Strathfield in the western suburbs of Sydney. Strathfield was then an old, well-established and rather prosperous suburb—the type of place one could be proud to live in. But we lived on the wrong side of the tracks.

Our home was on the northern side of Parramatta Road where the suburb was named Concord. There are various explanations of how that beautiful name was chosen. So much more poetic than the names of most of the inner suburbs of Sydney, taken from mansion-building colonial worthies. 'Concord' was reportedly either assigned because of an early peace agreement secured with the local Aboriginal inhabitants, or from the town in the United States, whose unpleasant revolution had led to the creation of the penal settlement at Sydney Cove. I never got to the bottom of the true explanation. Either account will do.

I have little recollection of my time under Mrs Church's tutelage. But I have it on the authority of my father that I was a quiet and studious boy with a joyful interest in creating objects with plasticine. It did not take me long to get the plasticine into my mouth only to discover that, although chewy, it was not edible. As the year wore on, I became keen to seek the limelight in the famous annual concert in which Mrs Church tried to demonstrate the beneficial effect on children that her little kindergarten was having.

Schooling with Mrs Church led naturally, on Sundays, to attending the adjacent church building, my earliest lessons in religion. No doubt that was how it was meant to be. The church was then described as belonging to the 'Church of England'. Only later was this association dropped in favour of the more impersonal designation, 'Anglican'. But above the altar of the church were two flags: the Union Jack and the Australian blue ensign. The name of the denomination might have changed, but the Englishness would always remain. There was also a lot of golden brass, polished so that it shone in the sunlight that seeped in azure hues into the church as we little children partook of early Sunday school. I had a Bible of my own, with lovely coloured plates. They illustrated the prophets of the Old Testament and the parables of the New. Jesus appeared in a coloured plate, with his kindly face. And like Mrs Church, Donald and Diana, his hair was fair. No visible freckles.

⁂

In December 1944, my days of kindergarten were over, and my mother took me in the following year to the closest public school. This was the infants' school at North Strathfield, a little more than a kilometre from our family home.

The infants' school building is still there in Links Avenue, so named because it abuts the golf links laid out in the early days of the suburb. The school is a two-storey building which looks as if it had been built in the 1920s. In 1944, like us the pupils, it still had the fresh bloom of youth upon it. The upstairs classrooms in particular were bright, and the large clear-glass windows meant that this was a sunny, well-lit, happy place. It was unlike so many other dark and pokey classrooms of the British Empire. On the walls were bright posters and a map of the empire on which the sun never set. Every land that was ruled by Britain was coloured in a lovely reddish hue, to distinguish it from the less attractive colours of more unfortunate nations. The French Empire, I remember, had a washed-out blue colouring. The

Dutch East Indies, just to the north of Australia, were painted yellow. This was, of course, a pre-war map. At the very time that I was admitted to the school, several of the pink-coloured lands, as well as those belonging to the French and the Dutch were occupied by our enemies. Little did we know then how quickly the great empires of earlier days would disappear, including our own reddish one: Britannia's dominions.

My teacher in Class 1A in the infants' school was Miss Pontifex. Like Mrs Church, she was tall. But she was always dressed in sombre colours and I remember that her hair was always tied in a neat bun. My daily journey to school took me along the suburban pathways of Concord. They were safe for walking. There was not much traffic in those days—a product of post-Depression austerity and wartime petrol rationing. Each day would commence with a school assembly that began punctually. And then all the children in Class 1A, mixed boys and girls, would march, just like our brave soldiers, up the concrete stairs with satchels in hand to the tune of the *Teddy Bears' Picnic*. The recorded band boomed out from the school loudspeakers and lasted until we were all safely in our seats in our classrooms. In those days, all the desks were in fixed positions, but with retractable seats. Some of the desks looked as if they dated from the time that the *Public Instruction Act* was adopted by the colonial parliament of New South Wales in the 1880s. Often there were carvings recording the names or initials of long-departed students. Never did I deface a desk in such a way. The very thought of doing so was shocking, even then, to my law-abiding nature.

Miss Pontifex's challenge was to teach us how to read and write. This meant learning the alphabet. The letters were already written on the blackboard in perfect copperplate style. First, the smaller version of 'a'. And then the larger. There were two measured lines across the blackboard within which the body of each letter was written. The slope of the writing, like our lives themselves, had to maintain a perfect and uniform forward tendency. The copperplate that Miss Pontifex taught us was graceful with lots of opportunities for curves and elegant decorations. This was not Miss Pontifex's objective. She simply wanted us to learn each of the letters of the alphabet and each of the numbers on the blackboard so that we could begin our journeys into literacy and numeracy.

The following year, 1945, was a big one in the history of Australia. It was the year we won the war. Australian soldiers had joined with others from Mother England, the United States and the Allied forces in the Pacific to defeat our enemies. These soldiers were out there in the jungles, faraway, helping to keep our peaceful suburbs, with their quiet homes and churches and schools, safe from foreign invaders. We all felt very grateful to them.

I remained in the infants' school in 1945. In Class 2A, my teacher for most of the year was Mrs See. She was less forbidding than Miss Pontifex. Miss Pontifex was condemned to go through life with the title of an imperial Roman leader, a title with which she seemed perfectly comfortable. Mrs See was more like one of the mothers. Shorter in stature, dressed in floral attire, more friendly. Still concentrating on reading and writing, but with a leavening of games. The year with Mrs See was more like my year with Mrs Church. She introduced us to a book, issued by the Department of Education, with simple stories designed to make our alphabetical studies more relevant. The book was distinctive because it had laminated paper and a special smell, unlike most of the coarse paper in those difficult wartime years.

Smells were important in the days of youth. My mother was a great gardener and I knew the smells of all the flowers that decorated the surrounds of our home. The vases in our living rooms displayed her best offerings. Nasturtiums, at the bottom of the garden, gave off a particularly memorable perfume. Whenever it returns, it takes me back to that small shaded part of my mother's garden in Concord. Roses and daphne might be more luxuriant, but my mother taught me also to love the strong earthy smells of chrysanthemums and dahlias.

∽

In 1946, I graduated from the infants' school to the 'big' school. This is still found on the corner of Concord Road and Correys Avenue in North Strathfield. Here indeed was a building erected soon after the passage of the *Public Instruction Act*. The school was the local physical symbol of the extension throughout New South Wales (and ultimately Australia) of the three great principles of public education: it would be free, compulsory and secular. Australia was the first continent on earth where every child would be educated in free schools. I was a beneficiary of this ambitious project.

Like public schools everywhere in the State, mine at North Strathfield had a badge in the form of a shield, which was coloured blue, with symbols I cannot now recall. For some reason, whilst the whole world called the suburb 'North Strathfield', the badge declared that we were 'Strathfield North PS'. And our school motto was 'Play the game'.

The school building had a large veranda at the front which faced Concord Road. In 1946, that road was not nearly as busy as it was later to become. However, I have clear memories of the large military trucks that passed like an ever-flowing stream along it. They were coloured khaki and on each side was a large white circle in which was emblazoned the sign of the Red Cross. These were the vehicles that carried the injured soldiers to the Concord Repatriation General Hospital, two kilometres along Concord Road at Yaralla. From time to time, we would be taken to stand at the front of the school building, or even on the footpath, to wave to dignitaries making the journey to the hospital. In the morning, if it was raining, I would arrive at the school on a double-decker bus along Concord Road. In those days, the buses were red, just like in England. The bus fare was a penny. Sometimes, despite the rain, I would walk to school so that I could purchase teeth-crunching hard-boiled lollies with that penny. Parents with triangular yellow flags stood guardian to halt the traffic, to let us pass safely into school.

In the 'big' school, boys and girls were separated. Girls were taught in the northern wing. In the southern wing, it was the boys. My classroom was under the charge of Mrs Godwin. By this stage, learning had become a much more serious business. Every student in Class 3A had to purchase a Commonwealth atlas. This had maps of the Australian Commonwealth, but also of the world in which we lived. Each month, every child in all of the state's public schools would receive the *School Magazine*. It contained stories and other items including poetry that could be used by the teachers in class. We were expected to read these out loud and would be marked when our moment came. The desks were still arranged in fixed positions, all turned towards Mrs Godwin, standing at the blackboard. When I was called upon to read, I would take the departmental magazine, stand in my place and recite the passage assigned to me.

We were also marked for writing. No ballpoints in those days. Instead, every desk had a hole cut out in one corner, into which was placed a white porcelain ink container. As if by magic, each night unknown emissaries of the Department of Education would appear to fill the containers. The school provided us with a brown wooden pen with a nib. If the nib was new, we had to suck it to give the ink traction so that it would flow freely. Slope cards were given to us to be placed under the pages of the green-covered departmental exercise books issued to us for writing. If we did particularly well in writing, or in presenting a little essay of our own, we were rewarded. Mrs Godwin would place a stamp in our book, which we could proudly show our parents. Invariably, the stamp was a red crown of St Edward. This was the crown our king wore. King George VI. We knew that he lived in England and that his soldiers had just won the war. As generally they did. How else did a quarter of the world end up coloured red?

It was in Mrs Godwin's class that I first became conscious of distinctive racial differences amongst our fellow students. One of the boys in my class was Bobby Chong, who had also come up from the infants' school. He was small in stature but, as it turned out, big in brain power. Before him lay a life of distinction in biology and, in due course, a professorial appointment in New Zealand. But, of course, we did not know that then.

I always tried to do my best in class. But Bobby Chong, from time to time, did better. These were the days of 'White Australia' and our classrooms, like the community generally, were pretty monochrome. We were mostly pale children who could trace our forebears to the British Isles. So Bobby's successes became doubly noticeable.

I remember an occasion in 1947 when I reported half-yearly results to my mother. It was in the garden at the front of our home in Concord. The one with the flowers. I handed my mother my report card signed by the Headmaster.

'I've got my half-yearly results, Mum.'

'How did you go?'

'Pretty well.'

'Where did you come?'

'Second in the class.'

'Who came first?'

'It was Bobby Chong.'

'Bobby Chong!'

Bobby 'McIntosh' or Bobby 'Yeomans' would have been unremarkable. After all, second in the class was not so bad. But in a country that still rejoiced in expelling Asian people, Bobby Chong's success came as something of a surprise. Years later, with other survivors of that class and our partners, Bobby Chong and I met again. The reunion took place in what in 1947 had been a grocer's shop but by then, symbolically enough, was a Chinese restaurant on the southern corner of Correys Avenue and Concord Road. We laughed about my mother's reaction, as she too would do in later years. We celebrated the progress that had come with the intervening decades. Today, Strathfield North PS has a large proportion of students who are Asian–Australians. Bobby was a standout in those postwar days. In more ways than one.

∽

In the following year, 1948, I moved to Class 4A and my teacher was Mr Casimir. He was a somewhat irascible man. He was forever going on about the evils of drinking and smoking. Because my parents neither drank alcohol nor smoked, these strictures did not affect me very much. However, in those days, more than 50 per cent of men in Australia did smoke. This meant that most of the boys in Class 4A would go home and tell their parents of Mr Casimir's rebuke for their having introduced the evil weed into the family. Looking back, he was ahead of his time. He was a good teacher and he made sure that we paid attention to the school broadcasts that interrupted the day from the wireless loudspeaker positioned at the front of the class, up near the ceiling.

The *School Magazine* contained the words of the songs we learned to sing in class. These were taught, over the radio, by Terence Hunt, a baritone with a splendid voice, strong and confident. Many of the songs, I recall, were traditional English songs with words that recounted the beauties of the scenery of Mother England. A favourite was *The Ash Grove*. But Terence Hunt was nothing if not eclectic. He also taught us *The Blacksmith*, with the powerful hammering theme that I was later to discover was one of the songs of Franz Schubert. A particular hymn we were taught, *These Things Shall Be*, was written by James Addington Symonds, a disciple of Charles Wesley. To this day, I can remember the words and tune. And the important message that it brought to that little classroom at North Strathfield:

> These things shall be, a loftier race
> Than all the world has known shall rise
> With flame of freedom in their souls
> And light of science in their eyes.

At a later hour, twice a week, we would all listen to an ABC radio broadcast by Mr H.D. Black on *The World We Live In*. He would always begin in his jaunty way, exclaiming, 'Hello girls and boys'. He would tell us about the events that had occurred in the preceding days, interpreting the great world happenings unfolding at that time so that we could understand them and see their relevance to our lives in faraway peaceful Australia. I can remember distinctly Mr Black telling us of the onward advance of the Red Army in China as it drove the forces of the Kuomintang to their ultimate exile in Formosa–Taiwan. The Chinese Revolution was underway. Whether it would bring riches to the Chinese people was of less significance, after the Japanese war, than whether it would bring danger to us in 'White Australia'.

H.D. Black later taught me economics at the University of Sydney. Later still, as Sir Hermann Black, he became Chancellor of the University of Sydney when I was appointed Chancellor of Macquarie University. In fact, he inaugurated me into that office. Macquarie University had been established in the 1960s at North Ryde, not so far from Strathfield North Public School.

Hermann Black on radio was a fine speaker and never boring. He believed in speaking quickly and never allowing his listeners to get drowsy with the message. I looked forward to his broadcasts, the drama that was unfolding, the outcome of which we did not then know. But somehow I felt confident that the King's forces would win through in the end against the assaults of all adversaries, just as sixteenth century Archbishop Thomas Cranmer's language in the *Book of Common Prayer* reassured us every Sunday at St Andrew's church.

Once a week, the entire school at Strathfield North would assemble in the courtyard of the playground. Occasionally, we would be taken off to a nearby park to plant trees on Arbor Day. This was a day designed to imprint on our minds the importance of trees, shelter and nature in the often harsh climate of Australia. I went back recently to the park where the trees I planted were. Sadly, they had not survived the burning heat of the intervening summers.

Sometimes at school we would be lectured by the members of the Gould League. They told us about birds and the beauty of the varieties of birds in Australia. Occasionally, there would be a talk from visiting lecturers about another kind of bird—gaol birds to be exact—in Australian history. Bushrangers, like Ned Kelly and Captain Moonlight, never failed to spark our childhood imaginations.

But always the school assembly would finish with the school song. They still have a school song at Strathfield North PS. But it is now different and not half as tuneful and optimistic as the one we cut our teeth on:

> Let us march in unison
> Let us do our best
> Face the world with eagerness
> Willing to stand the test.
> So here we stand, side by side
> Sturdy and strong together.
> Play the game
> On to fame
> Strathfield North forever.

Towards the end of 1948, two departmental officials in grey coats were introduced to the class by Mr Casimir. They handed out tests and we were given an hour to fill in the papers. I did so, little knowing the importance for my life of the outcome that would follow.

New South Wales, alone of the Australian States, had introduced a special State-wide system of education for so-called gifted and talented students. There were particular schools, like that attached to the Sydney Conservatorium of Music, for students wishing to specialise in music education. As well, there were a handful of schools that included classes for students judged as having a high IQ: 'Opportunity C Classes'. I simply filled in the form and thought nothing more of it. Then, in the post, came a letter from the Department of Education inviting my parents to arrange for me to attend for further testing on the top floor of its head office in Bridge Street in the city. This was an elimination round, designed to choose the best students from Strathfield North PS and other schools who would be given the chance of continuing their primary education at a selective school nearby. In my case, this was the Opportunity C Class at Summer Hill PS.

I made the grade. The invitation was extended and accepted by my parents. So, in 1949, I did not continue at Strathfield North. Henceforth, I would walk the long journey to Strathfield Railway Station to take up the rest of my primary education at Summer Hill PS, six kilometres from my home.

∽

The big public school at Summer Hill on Moonbie Street is still there, as is the large Moreton Bay fig tree in the front playground area. For most purposes, the school was then simply another local public school serving the surrounding suburbs. But within its grounds were the OC classrooms. The boys were separated from the girls. The classrooms themselves looked to date from the earliest days of the twentieth century. But into them came pupils from public schools in a dozen suburbs of Sydney, creamed off and chosen as a result of their IQ test performances. I cannot say that the change of school altered my attitude towards education or my own talents. I already knew that I was a high achiever, having beaten most of my peers except for Bobby Chong. In shifting to a new school, I just accepted the move as what was meant to be. Pride or self-satisfaction did not enter into the equation.

In 1949, my teacher in Class 5A was Mr Gorringe. I do not remember his first name but I recall that he lived at Yagoona, a suburb even more working class than Concord. In appearance, he was like a banker or economist. In those days, most male teachers wore suits and ties. Almost all of them displayed small lapel badges signifying their war service. As a teacher of the Opportunity C Class, Mr Gorringe was expected to give the students chosen for it greater chances to learn quickly and to indulge particular creative interests, such as drawing, painting and design. We were encouraged to draw, as our imagination took us, on the many blackboards that were provided. We were encouraged to take part in plays. As well, the OC curriculum allowed for increased numbers of visits to public institutions. We were taken on several school outings to Parliament House in Sydney. Regularly, we were observed by inspectors and teacher trainees as Mr Gorringe put us through our paces.

On one occasion I remember drawing in chalk a large illustration of what I thought Sydney would look like in fifty years. I provided for overhead roadways, towers and landing pads for planes. One day, I arrived at the class and to my surprise found that my masterpiece had been removed by an officious duster. Would that the product of my imagination had been photographed! It might have demonstrated that I had a lost vocation as an architect. Some of the glories-in-concrete that were later to spring up to deface the beauties of Sydney—the Cahill Expressway and the Western Distributor—were captured in my youthful depiction. Perhaps, after all, it is just as well that I turned to law.

Mr Gorringe encouraged our class to talk about the affairs of the world and of our nation. The year 1949 was one of big political changes. At the end of the previous year, the General Assembly of the United Nations, chaired by the Australian Minister for External Affairs, Dr H.V. Evatt, had adopted the Universal Declaration of Human Rights. This was explained to us by Mr Gorringe, with the aid of posters and photographs which were on display in our classroom throughout our time there. At a certain point, departmental officials came to the class to supplement Mr Gorringe's instruction. They handed each one of us a copy of the Declaration. It was memorable, again because of its paper. It was printed on airmail paper, doubtless because huge quantities of the document had been posted to every school in Australia. It was a great achievement of the United Nations, to which Dr Evatt had contributed. Mr Gorringe sought to explain to us that wars, like the Second World War from which Australia had just emerged, arose in part out of failures to accord people fundamental human rights. There were plenty of things for us to talk about in the classroom, including the apparent onrush of communism, the Berlin Blockade, the changes in China and the political challenges looming in our own country.

As the end of the year came closer, an announcement was made of the first federal election of which I was conscious. The Labor Government, led by Mr Ben Chifley—famously a train-engine driver—whose government had led the nation during the war, was looking tired and old-fashioned. A newly recreated personality, Mr Robert Menzies, was offering an attractive alternative. He promised to put 'value back in the pound'. He undertook to end the rationing of essential goods and clothing, notably petrol, that had commenced during the war. He said that he would give child endowment to the first-born child of

Australian families, hitherto denied benefits. As this meant me, I was naturally enthusiastic.

In our classroom, we were encouraged to debate all the subjects of politics and to express our views about them. Mr Gorringe, I can remember, was neutral and professional. Mr Menzies was duly elected in December 1949, and I recall that I was jubilant. My father was more cautious. One of the promises that the Menzies–Fadden Government had made during the election was to ban the Communist Party of Australia. My father's mother, my grandmother, had recently re-married. Her new husband was the national treasurer of that party. So my father was naturally worried about what this would mean for her and for her new husband, Jack Simpson.

Mr Chifley, with the rough voice, left office. The smooth-tongued Robert Menzies returned to power. A book was issued about the new members of the Federal Parliament. Somehow I acquired a copy—my father must have bought it for me. Thenceforth, I would sit with it listening to the broadcast debates of the Federal Parliament, to which we were often tuned at home, looking at the photos of all the members of the House of Representatives. My days of political consciousness had well and truly arrived.

The year 1949 concluded with a school performance of *The Mikado* by Gilbert and Sullivan. With all due modesty, I played the Emperor of Japan. My school friend, Graham Hill, later to be a judge of the Federal Court of Australia, played Katisha, the ugly daughter-in-law-elect. Other parts were played by Brian Spencer, who was later to be Registrar of Macquarie University when I was chancellor. Virtually every boy in that Summer Hill classroom went on to fame and fortune. Many are still my friends.

In 1950, in Class 6A our teacher was Mr Warren Tennant. By this stage I had reached a certain level of maturity—I at last knew my teacher's first name, although it would have been unthinkable to use it to his face. Mr Tennant was a handsome man and came from Merewether Beach, a suburb of Newcastle. But not far into the year, he was injured in a car accident that required his hospitalisation. He was temporarily replaced by the school headmaster, Mr Gibbons. He was a man of much greater age, having fought in the Great War of 1914–18. Mr Gibbons was not very happy about having been diverted from his tasks as headmaster of the entire Summer Hill School into teaching the precocious boys in the Opportunity Class. And he soon let us know his feelings.

We were all a bit frightened of Mr Gibbons. As headmaster, he came with a package. He was entitled to use the cane in the case of recalcitrant students. There was no appeal. He was a small, nuggetty man who packed a punch. This was expected of him. He had, after all, been one of the king's soldiers.

One difficulty with the porcelain inkwells in the school desks was that, occasionally, they could be displaced, causing their blue-black contents to spill everywhere. One fateful day, this happened to me. The ink went all over my precious exercise book. What a mess! There was nothing to do but tear out several pages that bore the offending ink stain. So this is what I did. That should have been the end of a trivial incident. Little did I know that Mr Gibbons was a vigilant guardian of the green of the Department of Education's exercise books—or that he had a perfect sense of weight. Later, on the day of the mishap, he picked up my book and felt that it was light of the expected contents.

'This book has had pages torn out of it.'

'But . . .'

It feels very light. You have torn out many pages.'

'But, but . . .'

'You have no right to purloin pages from the book.'

'But . . .'

'Don't you realise that this book is the King's property. You have destroyed part of the King's property. Come out front. You deserve two of the best.'

'But, but, but . . .'

'No buts about it. Hold out your hand.'

There was a swish of the cane. And then another before my sentence was discharged.

I had never been caned before. In fact, I had never before been disciplined at school. I had not needed it. I was the perfect little student, keen to learn and anxious to please. I sat disconsolately in my seat with the peculiar tingling feeling in my fingers that I can still recall. And the humiliation of it all. All I could do was to fervently hope that the handsome Mr Tennant would be back soon. He at least would have waited for my explanation. He would have accepted that my motives had been pure.

In due course, Warren Tennant resumed his duties and Mr Gibbons took himself and his cane back to his office in the front of the building, leaving the Opportunity Class to resume its civilised ways.

∽

In December 1950, the time came to leave primary school and to move schools once again. Endless forms had to be filled out, in which parents had to indicate their high school preferences. 'Fort Street Boys' High School', my mother wrote on the form in her beautiful copperplate handwriting that served as a model for my own. We all knew of the fame of that school, the oldest, continuously operating public school in Australia. It had been established in colonial times near the fort that protected the infant colony at Sydney Cove, up on Observatory Hill. The old school building, bearing the royal coat of arms, still exists close to the approaches to the Sydney Harbour Bridge that was built by Dr Bradfield in 1926. Back in 1950, that school building was still occupied by Fort Street Girls' High School.

Each of these schools was selective so that about three or four of the best students from the local public schools would be selected on the basis of their primary-school performances. Being the oldest public school, by 1950 Fort Street already boasted many of the most famous citizens of Australia amongst its alumni. They included Edmund Barton, the first prime minister, the Antarctic explorer Douglas Mawson and countless knights of the realm who had made good. In the political arena at the time, it was known that H.V. 'Bert' Evatt was a famous 'old boy'. On the other corner of politics stood a former premier of New South Wales, Bertram Stevens, and Percy Spender KC, earlier a minister in Mr Menzies' Government, and soon to become president of the World Court.

'What do you want as a present if you get to Fort Street?' my mother asked. I knew that my request had to be realistic for my parents were not well off. Yet I also knew that a lot was hanging on the decision. So I thought big; but not too big. 'Ten shillings!' I exclaimed.

And so it was that in an assembly of the whole of Summer Hill PS in December 1950, we gathered under the large Moreton Bay fig to hear the announcement of the selections for the departing students on their way to high school. The same Mr Gibbons arrived, this time without his cane. He read out the names. When he came to mine, I was full of apprehension.

'Michael Kirby. Fort Street Boys' High School.'

I had made it! My mother duly honoured her promise and presented me with a ten shilling bank note. It was coloured orange and brown and had an image of King George VI dressed in the impressive uniform of Admiral of the Fleet—just as a king should be.

The following year, it was to be the No. 459 bus—by now decorated in green—to Taverners Hill, Petersham, and the quest for excellence at Fort Street with its competitive motto *'Faber est quisque suae fortunae'*—every person is the maker of his own fortune.

∽

Looking back, I have to acknowledge that my parents were my greatest teachers, probably followed by my siblings and my grandmother, Norma. My father was always a great reader and storyteller. He would read us children the *Grimm's Fairy Tales*. Every night he would tell us stories of history and about books he had read or films he had seen. My mother was ambitious for our success at school without being overly zealous. She lifted my aspirations, telling me of her grandfather in Ulster, who had been a Fellow of the Royal Society of Ireland and of her great aunts who included a noted painter and botanist. We were very proud of these forebears—a cut above the rest.

Patiently, whilst forever ironing, my mother would listen as I told her what I had learned at school. She would correct and elaborate on my stories about the scribes of Egypt and the beginnings of the ancient civilisations of Mesopotamia. She would help me with spelling, always a weakness of mine. She would listen to songs that Terence Hunt had taught us. Once when I sang a Scottish song with my best attempt at a Scottish accent, I suddenly saw that she was crying. My imperfect efforts had reminded her of the Ulster accent of her father, William Spotswood Knowles, whom she loved and who had died in 1948.

Family apart, the debt to my teachers is enormous. I honour their memories. I wish that, in their lifetimes, I had thanked them personally. I remember them all as individuals. Without exception, they were devoted, accomplished and engaged with the students in their charge.

∽

I cannot bear to hear claims that public schools in Australia are 'light on values'. From my teachers I acquired a strong grounding in the values that underpin public education in Australia to this day. I learnt about democracy in a classroom of children from diverse backgrounds, economic circumstances and social attitudes. I experienced diversity, with fellow students of differing racial origins and religious traditions. I was shown enthusiasm with the joys of sport and games mixed deftly with the steady expansion of knowledge and the acquisition of the skills needed to help us in the journey through life. I was taught about excellence, with opportunities to maximise my talents and to pursue interests special to myself. I was introduced to secularism, and told about respect for the religions and beliefs of others.

Doubtless religious and private schools also boast of devoted teachers and great opportunities. But the chance I had to mix with so many children of different experiences was a very good grounding for me for the life that lay ahead. I will always acknowledge my debt to my teachers. Even Mr Gibbons taught me something: the sense of injustice that endures when decisions are made affecting others without giving them the opportunity to be heard.

In his poem *A School Song*, Rudyard Kipling, quite popular as a poet of the Empire of my youth, praised his teachers in words that I would use:

Bless and praise we famous men.
Men of little showing!
For their work continueth.
And their work continueth.
Broad and deep continueth.
Great beyond their knowing!

2

AFTER WOLFENDEN—HOW SCIENCE AND LAW CAME TO THE RESCUE

OVER FIFTY YEARS AGO, on 3 September 1957, when I was eighteen, Her Majesty's Stationery Office in London cranked out the report of the *Departmental Committee on Homosexual Offences and Prostitution.* This is usually known as the Wolfenden Report, after the chairman of the committee, Sir John (later Lord) Wolfenden. He was Vice-Chancellor of the University of Reading. Apparently he was chosen because of his reputation as a firm and effective chairman of troublesome committees. Wolfenden was a 'safe pair of hands'.

The committee was typical of the times in England. It comprised a High Court judge, a Foreign Office minister, a magistrate, a consultant psychiatrist, a professor of Moral Theology, a Scottish Presbyterian minister and the vice-president of the Glasgow Girl Guides. This diverse collection of the great and good first convened in 1954. In fact, creation of the committee was probably the result of an article, 'Law and Hypocrisy', published in the

Sunday Times in March 1954. That article attacked the outcome of the trial of Edward Montagu, the 3rd Baron Montagu of Beaulieu, and two other young men convicted of acts of sexual indecency with each other. Except that a lord was involved it is doubtful that the case would have been noticed.

Whilst the *Sunday Times* and other journals were critical of the conduct of police in the trial of the noble lord, some politicians and churchmen called for firm action to curb the spread of the 'detestable vice'. Medical researchers at the time described homosexuality as a severe mental sickness. Most observers of the British Establishment probably expected that the Wolfenden inquiry would touch lightly on its unpleasant subject matter and propose toughening the laws on the subject, or at least of holding the line.

In the result, however, the committee almost unanimously recommended that 'homosexual behaviour between consenting adults in private should no longer be a criminal offence'. Specifically, the committee found that 'homosexuality cannot legitimately be regarded as a disease, because in many cases it is the only symptom and is compatible with full mental health in other respects'. At the heart of the recommendations of Wolfenden and his motley band of colleagues was an idea about the limits of the law in enforcing personal morality in a free and modern society:

> [U]nless a deliberate attempt is to be made by a society, acting through the agency of the law, to equate the sphere of crime with that of sin, there must remain a realm of private morality and immorality which is, in brief and crude terms, not the law's business.

∽

The enactment of criminal offences against homosexuals in English law dated back to 1533. It was in that year that the parliament of Henry VIII first made 'buggery' a felony, punishable by hanging. Some unkind historians have suggested that this law was introduced as an aspect of Henry's great dispute with the Roman Church and in furtherance of His Majesty's design to get hold of the great wealth of the monasteries where the new offence could so easily be alleged, in order to strike terror in the hearts of the accused religious. Henry's law was soon repealed during the reign of his most Catholic daughter Mary.

The law was revived by the first Elizabeth, parliament complaining that Mary's repeal had emboldened 'evil disposed persons' to commit 'the said most horrible and detestable vice'. The ensuing language of statutory calumny survived in England for centuries, until ten years after the Wolfenden Report. Then, in the reign of the second Elizabeth, the 'abominable', 'detestable', 'unnatural' crime, which was 'so horrible as not to be spoken of amongst Christian people' finally departed the English statute book. What the codifier William Blackstone had extolled between 1765 and 1769, in his *Commentaries on the Laws of England*, and what the philosopher Jeremy Bentham (1748–1832) had mocked in his essay on legal reform, Wolfenden and his committee finally put to rest in twentieth-century England.

Bentham's distinguished disciple, John Stuart Mill, had propounded a general principle of lawmaking that found practical expression in the Wolfenden Report. Actions that were 'self-regarding' were not the law's business. Only actions that were 'other-regarding', particularly of the criminal kind, justified legal prescription. Actions did not become 'other-regarding' merely because they upset sensitive souls in society. The criminal law, with its heavy-handed punishments, stigma and shame, was not to be deployed on the basis only of scriptural texts and private sensibilities. 'Wolfenden & Co.' began a very important movement in the law of English-speaking countries to claw back the overreach of criminal law. The Wolfenden Report triggered a movement of law reform that led to reforming legislation first in England, then in Scotland, belatedly in Northern Ireland, in Canada and parts of the United States of America, in New Zealand, and, drip by slow drip, in the States of Australia beginning with Don Dunstan's reform in South Australia in 1975.

∾

It is probably hard for younger people today to imagine the atmosphere of the years before the Wolfenden reforms were enacted. But I can remember them. They were years of fear, fright and stigma. Hardly a week went by without the afternoon newspapers screaming their banner headline about 'perverts' being arrested. A young gay male coming to puberty in the Australia of the 1950s knew that there was a fair chance that he too could end up on the front page of the *Sun* or the *Mirror*. Famous visitors to Australia, like the great Chilean pianist Claudio Arrau, were fair game for police entrapment. The New South Wales Commissioner of Police, Colin Delaney, Australia's Father of the Year in 1960, proclaimed a campaign to protect society from this 'filthy vice'.

Governments in Australia regularly declared that homosexuals were a canker on the body politic and a terrible risk to national security. The strategies of fear and stigma drove even the bravest into silence. Silence from their families and loved ones. Silence even from themselves. All too often, the churches took their cue from the police and editorial denunciations. These were years when most gay men and women married, out of the expectations demanded of them. It was a cruel deception for their innocent partners. The venues for meeting other gays were few, often temporary and sometimes protected by real or suspected official corruption.

Gays were not, however, the only victims of this terror campaign: their families and friends were likewise shamed into silence. It was an age of shame and silence.

I know these things because the strategy I have described was targeted at me, personally. It worked. 'Don't ask, don't tell' was the price extracted to avoid the shame. Loneliness was the coinage in which the price of safety was paid. In my case, ferocious studies and numberless student committees were my distraction from the messages that the racing hormones were sending to my brain. It is difficult not to feel a bit resentful now about the cruelty of those hard times. As they were designed to do, the criminal laws inflicted their price not only on the 'perverts', who were heavily publicised once they had been arrested. The fear, stress and shame also drove all but the foolhardy into the closet where the door was shut, locked and barred. In 1950s in Australia, there was no apparent prospect of escape. But then came rays of light.

∽

In 1948, a decade before the Wolfenden Report, in the unlikely sleepy town of Bloomington, Indiana, a professor of zoology, Alfred Kinsey, diverted his scientific talents from a lifelong study of gall wasps to the taxonomy of sexual behaviour in human beings. From the unremarkable classification of his beloved insects, Kinsey began his trailblazing study of male sexual behaviour based on unique interview techniques designed to elicit what actually happened in human sexual conduct.

One of the early ideas that evolved from the thousands of interviews that Kinsey undertook was that the previous assumptions of a strict binary division between 'homosexuals' and 'heterosexuals' was factually inaccurate in the cohort of American mid-westerners surveyed. This led Kinsey to postulate a scale by which individuals could be ranked at different points in relation to their sexual behaviour, inclinations and interests. Kinsey's enterprise was not designed to collect erotic stories for the titillation of particular audiences. It was simply a taxonomist working with a new problem of classification. His methods remained much the same as with the wasps; only the subjects had changed.

Until Kinsey, there had been little wide-scale investigation of homosexual activity anywhere. In that respect, his research was unconventional and large scale. No one with such methodological precision had ever previously attempted a systematic study of human sexual experiences. When Kinsey's report was published in the United States, it created a storm. I was too young, at the age of nine, to remember those events of 1948. But in Australia, as in the United States, the storm continued well into the 1950s. It was reignited, with even greater media coverage, when Kinsey published his second report, in 1953, on female sexuality.

Kinsey's two reports challenged assumptions that were generally accepted throughout the world concerning human sexual activity. They demonstrated instead a widespread human inclination to sexual variety, experimentation and sexual experiences of various kinds throughout life. Yes, Kinsey's methodology can be criticised in the light of subsequent refinements of sampling techniques which improved in later studies. But clearly, Kinsey was onto some very important truths. Those truths were what hit the headlines in the 1950s.

I can remember the ambivalence of the media coverage of Kinsey in the Australian media at the time. By the publication of the female report, I was fourteen. Kinsey's findings challenged the denunciations of the 'perverts'. They showed remarkably high rates of homosexual experience amongst male Americans (at least 37 per cent with one overt same-sex experience to orgasm between the ages of sixteen and forty-five; lower amongst women). On balance, it seemed unlikely that things were very different in Australia. Naturally, with each year that passed, my eyes focussed whenever the media addressed the Kinsey reports and the lessons they seemed to convey for society and its laws.

Tucked away in the back of my mind was the reassuring insight that Kinsey's investigations appeared to convey. I was not alone. In fact, I was far from alone. In truth, there were many like me with same-sex attractions, including a sizeable number of bisexual people. The language of denunciation of the 'perverts', the police and governmental campaigns, and the instruments of shame and control were beginning to look a trifle unconvincing.

In the age of scientific miracles—of nuclear fission winning the war against Japan, of penicillin and the wonder drugs, and of the infant computers cracking the German codes—there was a growing confidence that scientific knowledge would always trump ignorance and superstition. Did this mean that the work of Kinsey and his followers would ultimately reveal that I was not 'evil' or 'perverted' after all? In my puzzled youthful mind, all of fourteen, I did not feel that wicked. I was just me, with my own feelings, kept quiet to myself. In the silence of my room, just before sleep, I would ponder and puzzle, then fret and attempt to work things out. But try as I might, I could not feel evil or perverted.

෨

I want to pay personal tribute to two great men of the twentieth century. Each was a child of the enlightenment. Each was a university scholar. Each in his different way contributed to the advancement of the human condition. Each, by different roads, added to society's wisdom and kindness. One—Kinsey—followed his path of scientific taxonomy in succession to his predecessors Havelock Ellis, Richard Krafft-Ebing and Sigmund Freud. The other—Wolfenden—followed his star of social science, in the footsteps of his predecessors Bentham and Mill. In combination, and with the works of the many who followed, these two men helped to initiate a major movement for law reform.

Their movement has not yet run its course—not by any means. In many countries, it has still had virtually no impact. But in the half century since the 1950s a remarkable change has been achieved in law, social attitudes and individual freedom in most of the countries, like Australia, that view themselves as part of Western civilisation. Even in such countries much remains to be done. Prejudice, discrimination, stigma and shame remain. Yet things are infinitely better because of Kinsey and Wolfenden and those who worked with and after them. More than half a century after Kinsey and Wolfenden, we should reflect on their ongoing impact on individual lives, on communal justice and the notion of mutual respect for each other's human dignity, which is the bedrock of human rights.

Of course, there are detractors of these men, their followers and their work. Kinsey is denounced as a biased observer, as a closet homosexual himself, and as a careless abuser of those whose interviews he conducted or planned and whose sexual 'misconduct' he viewed with neutrality and lack of proper outrage. Wolfenden is criticised because, as now appears to be the case, his son was homosexual. Seemingly, in the manner of the times, this had been kept a secret from him. In any case, Wolfenden could not have warped a whole committee including the Glasgow mistress of Girl Guides. If it were true that both Kinsey and Wolfenden were touched, then or later, by personal acquaintance with a subject of their investigations, this would leave their research, and the conclusions they drew, open to judgment on their merits. Or perhaps it would simply demonstrate the very incidence of the reality on which they were reporting.

The battalions of investigators into aspects of human sexuality that have followed Kinsey have finetuned his research findings. But they have not undermined the validity of his central discoveries. On the contrary, more recent research suggests the possibility of genetic and biological foundations for diversity in human sexual orientation. Likewise, Wolfenden's family encounter with homosexuality, if it occurred, is of trivial significance unless one subscribes to the preposterous suggestion that all that has flowed from the Wolfenden Report is the product of a worldwide gay conspiracy.

∽

In Australia, following the Wolfenden Report, the States and the two mainland federal Territories altered their laws on homosexual criminal offences. Effectively, they faced up to the reality of the diversity of human adult private sexuality taught by Kinsey. They accepted the instruction of Wolfenden and his colleagues that there was a 'realm of private morality and immorality which . . . in brief and crude terms, [was] not the law's business'. They copied the *English Reforming Act*, which itself had only just scraped through the British Parliament ten years after the Wolfenden Report. Step by step, as in England and elsewhere, Australian lawmakers lowered the age of consent. They removed the exceptions. Gradually they merged the sexual crimes against persons of the same sex as the perpetrator so that they became indistinguishable from the crimes committed by those of opposite sex.

One State alone in Australia held out against these reforms. Tasmania, the Apple Isle, resisted the change. Several attempts were made in the parliament of Tasmania to persuade the honourable members to change sections 122 and 123 of the *Criminal Code Act 1924* of the State. These were the provisions that prohibited sexual intercourse between males, and acts of gross indecency committed by one male with another. To a prosecution for such offences in Tasmania, it was no defence to prove that the conduct was carried on in private. Nor was it a defence to prove that both parties were of full age and understanding, capable of consenting to, and desirous of participating in the sexual activity concerned. These were the last Australian relics of the persecution of the 'abominable' crimes.

A final effort was made to push the offences from the Tasmanian statute book. It was attempted in terms of the urgent national effort to respond effectively to the AIDS epidemic. That strategy required lawmakers to do many unwished for things. These included permitting sterile needle exchange by injecting drug users to reduce the risks of HIV infection. There were other acts of courage. Removing the 'abominable crime' from Tasmania's statute book was, it was asserted, essential to tackle the risks of infection in the island state's gay community. The Legislative Council in its beautiful chamber in downtown Hobart remained unmoved. The democratic process in Tasmania had, it seemed, come to a full stop. Talk of Kinsey, Wolfenden and all their works fell on completely deaf ears.

At this time, two brave young Australians, Rodney Croome and Nicholas Toonen, asked me if they should lodge a complaint with the United Nations Human Rights Committee under the newly signed First Optional Protocol to the *International Covenant on Civil and Political Rights 1966*. Australia had agreed to be bound by the protocol on 25 December 1991, a Christmas present as Gareth Evans was to call it. Croome and Toonen wanted to argue that, by tolerating the continuation of the old crimes in Tasmania, the nation was in breach of its obligations under the covenant. I counselled against such a complaint. It did not seem timely. The Tasmanian law was not being vigorously enforced. The United Nations, I said, would never tackle such a sensitive topic. They should not waste their money and time. Famous last words.

Progress in human freedom belongs to the bold. In 1994 Nick Toonen took his case to the United Nations. He won. His decision stated a principle upholding sexual privacy amongst adults for the whole world. It offered the same rays of hope to gays into countries where homosexuality was oppressed that Kinsey and Wolfenden had brought. Those countries included oppressive, fanatical theocracies and cruel dictatorships. Sadly, they also included countries that share the British legal tradition and most of the countries of the new Commonwealth of Nations—in Africa, Asia and South America. These countries cling to the 'abominable' crimes. Like the English in the times of Henry VIII, they endlessly assert that homosexuality is a foreign import. That it does not exist within their cultures. That it is a corrupt Western practice. They defy the research of Kinsey. They reject the philosophy of Wolfenden.

In consequence of the Toonen decision, the Australian Parliament, with cross party support, enacted a federal law— the *Human Rights (Sexual Conduct) Act 1994* to override the last Tasmanian criminal offences that stigmatised Australian gays. Despite the passage of the federal law, the Tasmanian Parliament did nothing at first to repeal the offending sections of its Criminal Code.

Buoyed by their success in Geneva, Rodney Croome and Nick Toonen applied to the High Court, in 1997, for a judicial declaration that the State provisions were inconsistent with the new federal Act and, to that extent, invalid under the Australian Constitution. By this stage, I had been appointed to the High Court and took no part in the proceedings.

Tasmania asked the Court to rule on the suggested invalidity of the proceedings. Unanimously, it rejected that challenge. The Tasmanian Parliament quickly amended its law. The old 'abominable crimes' were removed from the Tasmanian statute book. Nowhere in the Australian Commonwealth do such crimes now remain.

⤜⤛

Changing criminal laws is one thing. Changing public attitudes is quite another. Continuing the momentum of change is also a very different matter. Extrapolating from the removal of criminal sanctions to the logical provision of equal civil rights is, for some, a bridge too far.

In many countries, including some that share the same legal tradition as Australia, important laws have been enacted to continue the lessons that Wolfenden and Kinsey taught. These include laws against discrimination against people for no reason other than their sexual orientation; laws providing equality of economic rights, including pension and superannuation benefits; and laws affording equal rights to an important civil status (such as marriage) or to recognised stable relationships (such as civil union). Now, with the same inexorable momentum as earlier demolished the irrational criminal laws against homosexual people, civil laws are being adopted or proposed to follow through the same logic. Sometimes these issues become instruments of wedge politics, religious intolerance, expressions of personal hatred and even instances of physical violence. But the caravan slowly and patiently moves on, teaching us to keep our eyes on the horizon. That way the big developments can be perceived and their directions predicted without forgetting where each little step must be made towards the distant goal.

The criminal laws of the past were often instruments of oppression. This was certainly true of the Nuremburg Laws imposed on the Jews in Nazi Germany. It was true of the Pass Laws addressed to 'black and coloured' people in pre-Mandela South Africa. It was true of Aboriginals and Asian immigrants in 'White Australia'. Before Wolfenden and Kinsey and their followers, it was true worldwide in the laws affecting homosexuals and other sexual minorities. In many parts of the world, those oppressive laws remain in place. In fact, some unjust laws are still in place in Australia. As a just people, we must resolve to remove them. Quickly.

∽

If I close my eyes, I am back in 1957, my first year in the Faculty of Law at the University of Sydney. I had finished my schooldays and was well and truly ensconced in university. I can still see

Mr Vernon Treatt QC coming to the stage of the Phillip Street Theatre where we took some of our lectures. Racy cabaret by night; legal lecture hall by day. Treatt's task was to instruct a hundred first year law students in that most important discipline, criminal law. I can see him toss his hat onto the chair, open his notes and begin reading his latest lesson. I can hear him talking about the sections of the *Crimes Act 1900* of New South Wales dealing with 'unnatural offences'. I can recall his rasping voice as he intoned the old provisions of section 79, spitting out the exceptionally ugly words of denunciation in the parliamentary prose: 'Whoever commits the abominable crime of buggery, or bestiality, with mankind, or with any animal, shall be liable to penal servitude for fourteen years.'

There, sitting on the strangely plush seats in the midst of all my university friends and colleagues, I felt the blood rushing to my face. I shuffled my papers. I looked down. Did any of them know, I asked myself. I hoped they could not guess. I could not bear the shame. I should be very, very quiet. Then, maybe, no one will ever know. No one will ever guess. I will get through life alone and sexless. But I would rather die than be seen on the front page of the *Mirror*.

These were the means by which law became an instrument, not of liberty but of oppression. Not of equality but of discrimination. Not of human happiness but of cruelty and unkindness.

Whenever I hear about the 'good old days' in the law, I think of that lecture hall. Then my mind switches to the people who helped release me, personally, from that oppression. People like John Wolfenden. And Alfred Kinsey. People like the politicians of both major parties in Britain and Australia who introduced and enacted the changes. And I also remember those who stood against the changes. Some still do.

*

The important lesson of this story travels far from London, where Wolfenden wrote his report or Bloomington where Kinsey worked on his taxonomies. It goes far from Australia and the Apple Isle, and from Geneva where the Human Rights Committee upheld Nick Toonen's complaint, astonishing me and many others. It goes to Singapore where the Law Society urged the repeal of the 'unnatural offences' and caused Lee Kuan Yew to declare: 'Let's not go around like this moral police . . . barging into people's rooms. That's not our business.' It travels to Zimbabwe where gays and others are oppressed, causing Bishop Desmond Tutu to explain that penalising someone for their sexual orientation 'is the same as penalising someone for something they can do nothing about, like ethnicity or race'. It goes to the largest democracy in the world, India, where in 2009 the Delhi High Court invalidated the application to consenting adults in private of the old British law against homosexual activity. Some politicians and moralists still cling to the old British laws, although they have no roots in India's Hindu tradition and are denounced by Amartya Sen, the Indian Nobel Laureate, as 'archaic and brutal [serving] to persecute, blackmail, arrest and terrorise sexual minorities'.

In every land, but especially beyond the West, the old laws of internalising shame and oppression remain steadfastly unmoved. The lesson of the Wolfenden Report is that efforts are needed beyond the West. We must bring to lands far away and close to home the wisdom and justice of Wolfenden and of the scientific discoveries of Kinsey. We must do so for every vulnerable group that is oppressed whether they be women, children, the old, the young, racial minorities, religious minorities, sexual minorities. More than fifty years after Wolfenden, the greatest challenges for human dignity still lie ahead. The oppression I have described should be confronted as part of the global response to HIV and AIDS. More importantly, it should be confronted to expand respect for the freedom of everyone who is now oppressed.

Half a century after the judge, the magistrate, the Girl Guide mistress and the academic surprised themselves, Britain and the world, by producing the Wolfenden Report, we should honour its authors and the 'safe hands' that steered their work to success. Kinsey laid the ground and prepared the way. Many champions who have followed have turned the Wolfenden ideas into action. Some things are indeed 'not the law's business'. Those who cherish liberty and human progress must be bold and insistent in saying so. Not just in Australia. Everywhere. It's a basic question of justice. And of decency to one another.

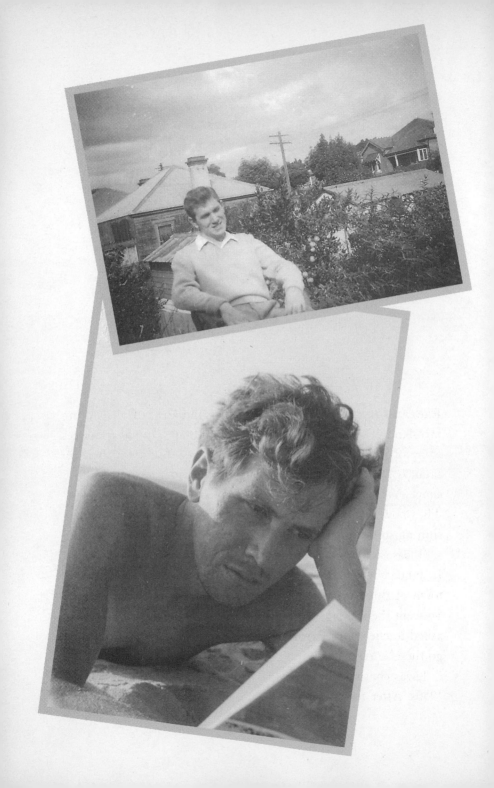

3

MY FRIEND JIMMY DEAN—
A NOSTALGIC JOURNEY

EXCEPT FOR A FEW hills in the south, Indiana is flat. Rolling farmland of the mid-west of the United States, it still produces some of the best corn in the world. When I arrived there in January 2000 the land was already covered in a deep blanket of snow. As the car hurried north to Fairmount a full moon rose. The snow reflected the moon's sharp light. Mile after mile of shining snow.

'Please tell your client that there is nothing in Fairmount. In January there is no ground transport. No taxis. It is a little town of three thousand. They have nothing but James Dean.' So went the message to the travel agent in Sydney whom I had asked to check out Fairmount, Indiana. 'Do you really want to go there?' 'Yes I do.'

I was chasing a memory of Jimmy Dean. A memory of the 1950s. After forty hours of flying and some of the worst snow storms for years, I was finally in the car on the way to James Dean's home town.

'It will take us three hours to get there,' said the car driver. 'That's surprising,' I said. 'The travel agent said that it would only take an hour and a quarter.' 'Well, to tell the truth, I've never been there. I've gone past it a few times and seen the sign to Fairmount. But I've never actually driven there, so they may be right,' she conceded.

As the car sped along I tried to imagine a Sydney taxi driver being unaware of how long a journey would take an hour or so from Sydney airport. I was lost in my thoughts as the little towns appeared and quickly disappeared. More snow.

An hour and a quarter, on the dot, the sign said 'Fairmount'. 'They were right. Well, whaddya know?' the driver drawled. Off the highway we went. Now we were really in the farming countryside. A featureless narrow road took a track in the direction of Fairmount. Before long we reached a junction. To one side was the town. To the other side (as I was to discover) was James Dean territory. And also the bed-and-breakfast residence at which I was to spend the night. There are still no hotels or motels in Fairmount. Only Mrs Loften's house in which she occasionally receives overnight visitors in search of Jimmy Dean.

Because of the snow storms I was about three hours late. Not much in terms of crossing the world. But my mind began to consider what I would do if Mrs Loften's lights were out and the shutters barred. 'I don't imagine they get many visitors here in January,' said the driver reassuringly.

Along a still narrower road we drove past a cemetery. Perhaps that's where Jimmy Dean lies buried, I thought. Then, on the left, set back well from the road, appeared a kind of country farmhouse. This was the Loft Inn. Happily the lights were still burning. The car swung into the drive and found the entrance at the rear. I picked up my bag and felt the cold blast of Indiana winter. It was an hour or so short of midnight. Mrs Loften, a quiet reserved woman of middle years, showed me to the front bedroom. Everything smelt so clean. The bed was soft and the combined effect of the long hours of travelling and the safe arrival at my destination soon carried me off to sleep. But just before I shut my eyes I noticed on the wall of the bedroom, in English and in German, a prayer of the Lutheran pastor Dietrich Bonhoeffer, murdered by Hitler. The message was simple: 'May God give us the grace to rise above our failings; to hate no one; and to show love to our enemies.'

⁊

In 1955 it was hard growing up gay in Sydney, Australia. It cas still be hard—anywhere. But those were the days of Police Commissioner Delaney, police harassment, criminal punishment and widespread religious intolerance. Homosexuality, pre-Wolfenden, was still the love that dared not speak its name. The subject was taboo in suburban Australia. At my all boys' school no one talked of sexuality, unless it was to denigrate the 'poofters' or to heap contempt on a fellow student who showed as much as the slightest hint of sensitivity. 'Queer as a witch's ear' was the way that kind of behaviour was denounced, to gales of confident schoolboy laughter.

When I was fifteen I was full of confusion about my feelings. Every message I received told me that they should be a source of deep shame. In those days no one talked about 'gay rights'. Religion, law and society insisted that you hold your tongue. It was to be fifteen more years before I would reveal all to my family—and receive in return their loving support. But in 1955 that part of my life was secret. If you were gay, your emotional life was covered in a blanket of silence as thick as Indiana snow.

Into this lonely world came an image. By chance I saw the new Elia Kazan movie *East of Eden*. I cannot now remember whether it was at the Strathfield Melba, the Concord Ritz or the Concord West Odeon. Maybe it was in the city. Sitting there in the cinema, watching the new American movie star James Dean, I felt identification. Perhaps the presidential candidate John McCain was right, after all, when he told the American people that in the military you develop an instinct to detect someone who is sexually ambivalent. 'Gaydar', as the US weeklies describe his remarkable skills of detection. Well my 'gaydar' must have been working in overdrive in 1955 when *East of Eden* hit the movie houses of Sydney.

James Dean was twenty-three when he played Cal Trask in the movie version of John Steinbeck's novel of the same name. It was a story of a young man's quest for love, acceptance and identity. It was not a gay story—far from it. In those days that would have been impossible for Hollywood. But something about the young Dean spoke to me in the dark cinema. For a few months I developed an obsession about him and the movie. Most unusual for me. Generally, at that time and since, I have held in a kind of contempt the Hollywood groupies whose lives turn on the flickering images of their celluloid heroes and heroines.

So affected was I by *East of Eden* that I saw the movie over and over again as the film did the tour of the Sydney suburbs. I simply followed behind. From the Canterbury Palace to the Gymea Lyric, I queued up and sat in the back stalls watching again the images of the sunny Salinas farmland in California, listening to the lovely music of Leonard Rosenman and sinking into the fantasy world that James Dean inhabited.

I went to suburbs of Sydney that I did not even know existed. Having no car, I travelled around by public bus and train. On warm nights and cold nights I was there, watching the screen and feeling once more the emotions summed up by the movie. Looking back, it seems a trifle weird. Today, I usually find it difficult to sit through a movie once. Yet I saw *East of Eden* twenty-four times. Fortunately, I never formed the same attachment to Dean's other movies, *Rebel Without a Cause* and *Giant,* released after his death. In fact, they both left me rather cold. I saw them once and once was enough. But *East of Eden* was then, and has remained since, special. In 1955, my brothers and sister put my devotion down to some quaint eccentricity. They were used to peculiarities in their elder brother. No one would have been so rude as to interrogate me about the real cause. This was just Michael's magnificent obsession. It would pass.

On 30 September 1955, at a time that I was studying for the Leaving Certificate at the end of my high school days, James Dean was killed when his Porsche 550 Spyder crashed on Route 466 in southern California. The young actor was dead at twenty-four, his neck broken, his already famous features shattered. The news of his death, filtering down to summertime Australia, merely reinforced my feelings about him. It seemed the inevitable outcome to loneliness and sensitivity—an early death. What a waste.

'What would you say about a person who saw *East of Eden* twenty-four times?' a colleague in my first year at university asked a postgraduate friend studying psychology. 'I'd say that that person was in love with James Dean,' she answered, quick as a flash. My colleague looked at me. Awkward silence. I reddened and muttered a few feeble excuses. In those days it was dangerous to be caught out as homosexual. I tried to throw sand into the eyes of my staring interrogators. Further silence. Of course, the psychology major had put her finger on the truth. Deprived of the adventures of teenage love, I had to find my fantasies on the cinema screen. So Jimmy Dean became a kind of love. Like most obsessive loves, it was to pass. Time and maturity would replace the flickering image of a dead actor with the reality of human beings.

But Jimmy Dean always remained there, treasured as a recollection of lonely times growing up gay. If I saw his photo or caught a re-run on late night television, the memories of 1955 would come flooding back. In Canterbury and Gymea the cinemas are now closed. Furniture stores or carparks take the place of most of those dark halls in which I saw *East of Eden* as it toured Sydney in the mid-1950s. Yet the memory is still there waiting to be summoned forth. Music could always do it. At Christmas in 1956, my brother Donald had given me a microgroove recording with the music from the three James Dean movies purchased from his pocket money. When we put on the record and it played the stirring theme by Rosenman that opens *East of Eden*, I burst into tears. When at Christmas 1999 he gave me a new recording on CD of the same music, there were no tears left. Just a sense of sadness and loss which I suppose everyone feels about loves faraway and long ago. The real and the fantasy worlds merge together and become almost indistinguishable. Somehow I felt I had known Jimmy Dean. But that was eons ago, when I was lonely. Then he seemed to speak to me.

∽

James Byron Dean was born in Marion, Indiana, on 8 February 1931. His father, Winton Dean, was a dental technician, described as a dutiful parent but rather remote and humourless. His mother, born Mildred Wilson, locked in an indifferent marriage, tried to enliven the chores of motherhood in Marion and Fairmount, Indiana, with poetry reading and a keen interest in the school pageants of her only son.

The young James grew up in Jonesboro, a few miles from Fairmount, until he was five years of age when, in 1936, his father received a government appointment in California. The family moved there. However, in 1941, Mildred Dean died of cancer. In an essay written at the Fairmount High School a few years later, the young James expressed his anguish: 'I never knew the reason for Mom's death, in fact it still preys on my mind.'

Dean's father felt unable to rear his young son in California. So he sent him back in a train to Fairmount to the mother's sister, Ortense, who had married Marcus Winslow. They then had no children. They lived on a farm and agreed to bring up Jimmy Dean as their own son. The young boy travelled alone across America, his mother's coffin going with him in the goods wagon. Family legend records how, at every prolonged stop, the young James would run back to that wagon to make sure that his mother's coffin was still there.

The Winslows, like many of the people in Jonesboro and Fairmount, were Quakers. They owned a medium-sized farm just down the road from what became the Loft Inn. Jimmy slept in the upstairs front bedroom. He went to the local schools. He hung around the bicycle shop where he would occasionally see the latest motorbikes. He came under the influence of a Wesleyan minister, the oft-questioned James De Weerd. A few years after his arrival, as sometimes happens, the childless Ortense gave birth to Marcus Jr, James Dean's cousin. They were to grow up together.

There were not too many Roman Catholics in this part of the United States. Virtually no Jews, few blacks. Northern Indiana had a large population of German descendants. Not a few of the largest farms were owned by the Amish, refugees from the errors of a naughty world. In summer it was hot and the corn grew. In winter, snow. At the Fairmount High School, James Dean excelled in basketball and drama. The former was surprising because, in the words of one who knew him, he was 'blind as a bat' without his glasses. But he was determined to succeed. His interest in drama was encouraged by one of those necessary chances in life—an inspired teacher who saw his potential and tried to make the most of it. This was Miss Adeline Nall. The first time the young James strode the boards was in the school hall at Fairmount High. Miss Nall took him throughout the State to oratory and speaking competitions where he sometimes did well. She fostered in him the idea that in the world of imagination and drama, he could not only escape the flat plains of Fairmount, but maybe also the memories of the loss of his mother. Dean did not forget his first mentor. In early 1955 he invited Miss Nall to join him for a screening preview of *East of Eden* in the state capital, Indianapolis. You can imagine her pride in her pupil made good.

At the end of his schooldays, James Dean went first to New York and then to California to seek his fortune on stage and screen. And so it was that Jimmy Dean went back to his father who had remarried in California and with thousands of others searched for a chance in Hollywood. As a carpark attendant he met and befriended a young businessman from the East Coast who promised him contacts in New York. Some form of sexual liaison appeared to have followed. Did it matter? The result was that James Dean, a late teenager, was accepted into the famous Actors' Studio in New York, which had produced Marlon Brando and many other stars. He began to win bit parts in the new world of television commercials, and in Broadway plays. The reviews were good and he was making more contacts. Eventually his friends secured him screen tests for the lead role with Julie Harris in Elia Kazan's *East of Eden*. Kazan with Harris, already one of America's most respected actresses, ensured that the movie would have high dramatic standards. Dean was just made for the part of Cal Trask. In some ways the story, which involved the early loss of a mother and a quest for the love of his father, was just made for James Dean. The emotions were pure and natural for him. The screenplay must have appeared semi-autobiographical. Maybe that explains the power of his performance.

Dean's death in September 1955, immediately after the successful premier of *East of Eden* and on the eve of the release of the two later films, ensured his immediate canonisation by the public relations machine of Warner Brothers Pictures. After the crash, Winton Dean brought his son's body back to Fairmount— the second time a family coffin had crossed the United States from California. There, in early October 1955, James Byron Dean was buried in a rear lot of the local cemetery. His resting place was less than a mile from the farmhouse in which he had grown up. As the Reverend De Weerd said at the large funeral service held at the Friends' Meeting House in Fairmount, Jimmy was not coming home to Fairmount—as far as Fairmount was concerned, he had never left.

Mrs Loften woke me at eight in the morning. A large breakfast was laid out for her solitary guest. Now I knew what an American breakfast really meant. At nine o'clock Phil Zeigler arrived. He was to be my guide through James Dean territory. My visit to Indiana had been arranged by Indiana University, a distinguished institution with a big legal faculty. I had been invited to inaugurate a new professorial chair of law. Bemused, my hosts were willing to go along with the unusual request of this visiting Australian judge. If Fairmount I wanted, Fairmount I would have. They had contacted the Fairmount Historical Museum. Phil Zeigler, a bluff, enthusiastic devotee of James Dean and all his works, was the honorary custodian.

As soon as we got in the car to drive to the museum, Phil told me that he had fought in Korea alongside Australian soldiers and found himself in trouble when he tried, out of turn, to shout the Aussies a beer. He almost made it to Australia once. There was a competition between US ships for recreation leave in Sydney. Somehow in firing practice another ship had won the call so Phil had never been Down Under. But he admired the Australian soldier. He was only too happy to show this Australian visitor around Fairmount, especially because we shared a devotion to Jimmy Dean.

We left the Loft Inn and retraced the narrow road back to the town. Fairmount is a small place. It probably hadn't changed much since James Dean's time. On every second corner there seemed to be a Protestant church. But the Friends' Meeting House was the biggest place of worship in town. The historical museum stood on a corner which was completely snowed in. A path had been cleared and Phil led me into the museum itself. It was packed with memorabilia of the most famous son of Fairmount.

In one cupboard were items of James Dean's property and photos showing him with them. Baby clothes. The old fashioned tape recorder he used with his bongo drums. The watch he wore in a movie still. A card showing a dental appointment in the week after he was killed. His spectacles and a travelling shaving kit. The marked-up script of *Giant*. A letter to him from Edna Ferber, the author of the book on which that last movie was based. Contracts with Warner Bros signed by Dean. Posters and movie stills from his three major films. A legal document evidencing his acquisition of an apartment in California. A leather jacket which showed quite clearly what a small man he had been.

Phil left me alone with my thoughts as I looked at these objects and tried to take my mind back to the mid-1950s half a world away. I was in the middle of examining the school photos from the Fairmount High when my reverie was broken by the appearance of Marcus Winslow Jr, James Dean's cousin. He was a few years younger than I, still a handsome man with a square jaw and steady gaze. He had that reserve which I knew well from my mother's side of my family. It is a feature of the Irish people from Ulster. The Winslows and the Deans, it seemed, came to America with the Pilgrim Fathers and other Quaker refugees from religious persecution in England.

I saw Marcus sizing me up as he looked at this stranger from *terra incognita*. Doubtless he wondered what had brought me to Fairmount in January. But neither he nor Phil Zeigler were impolite enough to ask. That would probably have happened in New York or New Jersey. Almost certainly in California. But not in Fairmount, Indiana. There you kept your psychological distance. He answered my questions. He did not unnecessarily volunteer information. A perfect courtroom witness, I thought to myself.

I showed Marcus an extract from a book about James Dean. It described the way Marcus' parents had looked after Dean for nearly ten years. He recalled those years, describing his close brotherly friendship with the famous actor. Somehow I did not know how to describe his cousin in the conversation. Calling him 'Jimmy' seemed too familiar in the company of a relative who doubtless called him just that. Yet calling him 'James Dean' seemed untrue to my own imaginary association with this person who was flesh and blood in Marcus Jr's memory. So I ended up with circumlocution. Most of the time I did not really call him anything. This person who had brought me to Fairmount and us together was, in his different ways, vivid and present in the museum, surrounded by the bric-a-brac of his life.

'You must have passed inspection,' Phil announced to me later. 'He's invited you out to the farm. You can have a look at Jimmy's motorbike. It is usually here. But Markie is taking it down to Independence, Missouri. They want to borrow it for an exhibition at the Harry S. Truman Museum there.'

Perhaps I had passed inspection because of the element of reserve in my own nature. But I was glad to be invited to the Winslow farm. It would take me to a place where Jimmy Dean lived and breathed the air, and experienced Januarys which were as cold as this. So Phil drove his car back along the road towards the Winslow farm. On the way he showed me the Wesleyan church where the Reverend De Weerd had regaled the young Dean with his dramatic sermons. He showed me the Friends' Meeting House where the funeral service had been held in October 1955. We passed again the Loft Inn set back from the road and the cemetery. And there was the Winslow farm. Jimmy Dean had written how he had worked on the farm only when somebody was watching him. At all other times he had fled into his mind and escaped to the world of his own imagination.

At the farm Phil pointed out the upstairs front bedroom in which Jimmy Dean had slept. 'I slept in that bed myself once,' he said proudly. That was an eerie thought. My imagination played tricks with it. It is one thing to be in celluloid and on the silver screen. It would be another to be a live human being sleeping in that upstairs bedroom in a farmhouse in the middle of almost nowhere.

In the garage adjoining the Winslow farm was a trailer. In the trailer was Jimmy Dean's large British motorcycle. Marcus pointed to its features. It was top of the range in 1955. Early in the year Jimmy had come back to Fairmount, covered with laurels as *East of Eden* had opened throughout the United States. That was the last time he was to see Fairmount alive. 'He loved that bike. You can climb in there and have a closer look at it if you like,' Marcus offered. I resisted the invitation. Speed has never been a big thing with me. Fast cars and motorbikes were Jimmy Dean's eventual undoing. Yet this was part of his world of escape and I thought of that as I looked at the bike in pristine condition in the Winslow trailer awaiting its journey south.

'Will you get somebody to take it down to Independence?' I asked.

'No way!' Marcus would not trust anyone else with this precious item of his famous cousin's life. He would drive down himself taking two days and, in due course, fetch it back. It would be returned to the Fairmount Historical Museum. Phil Zeigler would resume charge of it.

Phil offered to show me other places around the farm with memories of Jimmy. But there was a metre of snow in most parts and it was difficult to get about. My city shoes were not entirely suitable, so we called off the walk in the garden. 'We'll go and see the cemetery,' said Marcus. He was a man of few words and I liked him. He seemed to tolerate his visitor from faraway. He had never been to Australia. And from his responses I gathered that this son of Fairmount had no great desire to see it now. 'If you come, look me up,' I said, giving him a card. He thanked me politely. Politeness and good manners are the passport to acceptance in the American mid-west.

We drove back along the straight road and into the cemetery. There Marcus stopped in front of the graves of his parents, Ortense and Marcus Sr who rest on one side of James Dean. On the other side lies James' father and his second wife. James's much loved mother is buried a few miles away in Marion.

Because of my shoes it seemed impossible to get out into the snow to view the grave. But I was determined. I had not come this far to drive away without paying my respects.

'Hold on. I'll make some footsteps for you,' Phil said. He leapt out of the car. With his boots he walked around to my side of the car and back again, stamping footprints in the snow to the edge of Jimmy Dean's grave. I could see that this was the action of a person who understood my need to just stand there. Who knows the reasons for Phil Zeigler's love of Jimmy Dean? Who knows the reasons of the thousands who come to Fairmount every year and stand in this place, lost in their own thoughts?

I stood quietly at the grave. And I thought of Ortense and her husband who had taken on the responsibility of bringing up this gifted and difficult child. I walked over, without benefit of footprints, to Marcus's car. I told him that I had paid my respects to his parents. He thanked me and shook my hand. He then drove off.

Phil took me back into town where I discovered that Marcus Winslow was a major figure in the business world of Fairmount. He had bought the bicycle and motor shop down the road where young Jimmy used to hang out as a teenager. We pulled up at a large garage. Marcus reappeared and showed me the motor cars that had been associated with Jimmy Dean when he lived in Fairmount. There was no sign of the Porsche in which he had been killed. It disintegrated in the crash, its parts scattered to the winds. But there was the car—all chrome and duco—the young James Dean had driven to the Fairmount High School. Huge posters lined the garage walls. Many of them were from foreign-language versions of Dean's three films, some with titles significantly changed, especially *Rebel Without a Cause*, which presumably did not translate well into French or Spanish. Proudly displayed on the wall of the back room office was the first day cover of the stamp bearing the image of James Dean issued by the US Post Office. 'We thought it should have been issued first in Fairmount. But under the pressure of the film studios, they issued it first in Hollywood,' Phil Zeigler explained. 'That's big business for you,' he sighed. Models of the Porsche were in the office. This I found hard to understand, but people in farmland USA love their cars. Jimmy Dean was no exception.

I shook Marcus Winslow's hand for the last time. 'Come again,' he said. 'Next time come in the summer'.

Phil and I drove off to The Legend, the only diner in Fairmount. It had remained much the same as it was in James Dean's day, its walls covered with movie photos of Dean. There, waiting for us, was the manager, a young woman known as 'Lady' and her assistant, Dan. Normally shut on Mondays, Lady and Dan opened up just for me. It was warm inside. Dan had turned on the grill in case we wanted some lunch. I decided that this was the time for an American hamburger, which I ate in those days. Lady offered Dan the only apron that was available—a pink one. Dan was not going to have any of that. 'You're not a pinko,' said Phil. 'No way,' confirmed Dan. Dan, it appears, had once been a policeman. There was nothing pink about him—either politically or sexually. There was no way he was going to wear a pink apron, especially in front of a foreign guest.

As we ate Phil told me of the James Dean celebrations that take place in Fairmount every September to commemorate the actor's death with visitors coming from far and wide, packing out the hotels and motels for miles around. His movies are shown and his images remembered, but most people who come are, it seems, car fanatics. They bring their vintage cars, relics of the 1950s, hold a big rally, inspect the Winslow car museum, and visit the graveside. Television stations have tried to take over the grave site to the great annoyance of the large crowd of fans who walk with ceremonial dignity from the memorial service at the Friends' Meeting House along the narrow road to the cemetery.

There is also a 'James Dean look-alike competition', in which even Dan had taken part. I stole a look at the hamburger cook, trying to hide my disbelief. It must have been many years ago, I thought to myself. Dan had his own kind of beauty, but in all truth, it was nothing like James Dean's.

'They take that competition very seriously,' Phil explained. There was one guy who kept coming back. He was not a bad likeness. But there were several who were better. This guy protested when he was rejected for the second time. He kept making trouble. But we have some pretty reliable judges. They include people who knew Jimmy at school and who grew up with him here. They come along every year. Sometimes they say that it is uncanny. On one occasion the winner was the spitting image of James Dean. It was just astonishing. Some entrants come from Mexico. Some come from further afield.'

Elvis competitions were all the rage in Thailand, I told Phil. Asian Elvises had been popping up everywhere. Some people say Elvis never really died. Phil nodded with understanding. He took me over to the wall where the photographs of the James Dean look-alikes hung. They did not resemble the James Dean of my memories, of 1955 Sydney. There was a photo of Phil in army uniform just out of Korea. He was handsome—almost dazzlingly so. I told him this. He seemed quite pleased. The ravages of time had taken their toll on both Phil and me, but the legend of James Dean lives on, as beautiful and as vulnerable as he was.

We finished our hamburgers and fries, a jukebox played the music of the 1950s. A car was waiting to take me to the Indiana University and Phil, in the best German tradition of his ancestors, was getting nervous that we were keeping the driver waiting. 'Let him wait,' I said. I thanked Lady and Dan and they presented me with a gift—a bottle of Coke of the kind sold in 1955 wrapped in a cotton serviette from The Legend. They would take no money for the hamburgers. As I left they locked the door.

On the way out of the town we drove past the old Fairmount High School where James Dean received drama lessons from Miss Nall. Despite its famous alumnus the school was empty, the building derelict and many of its windows broken. Students are now sent to a regional high school out of town.

At the Loft Inn I bade farewell to Mrs Loften and my guide—a generous-spirited American who had put himself out for no reason other than our common bond in James Dean. He seemed pleased that I had come along. 'We don't get many people between September and March,' he said. Then he drove away and I returned from the world of my past to the world of the law and universities.

❧

Indiana University has always been a place of ideas, sometimes to the discomfort of the farming state in which it is so securely placed. Its president for many years was Dr Herman Wells, a remarkable man who supported independent thinking and resisted the waves of populist passion that have passed over modern Indiana and the United States from time to time. The university backed staff and supported academic freedom during the worst doings of the McCarthy years. It is still battling with those who want to close down the Kinsey Institute, housed in the university. It was here in the 1940s, at the time James Dean was growing up in Fairmont, that Dr Alfred Kinsey conducted his research on sexuality in the American male. That research is still controversial today.

I saw some of the archives of Dr Kinsey's work while I was at the university. The institute's struggle to make normal the great variety of human emotional and sexual experience is not over. Its director told me of attempts in the Indiana legislature to stop its ongoing investigations of human sexuality. In the heartland of the American mid-west there are still some who condemn any sexual difference as unspeakable. As far as the Kinsey Institute and Dr Wells—and his successors in Indiana University today—were concerned this question was scientific. It was one for empirical research. Truth is the great flame that lights the way. Indiana University is a keeper of that flame.

I had written from Australia to seek an opportunity to speak to the student members of OUT—Indiana University's lesbian and gay students' association. They told me of the difficulties of growing up gay in the mid-west of the United States in 2000. 'Don't ask don't tell' was still the rule. How very much like suburban Sydney in the mid 1950s, I thought.

∽

On the plane home from snowy Indiana to summertime Australia I thought about my visit to Fairmount. Images kept returning to my mind. The cemetery. The museum, The Legend and all the people I had met. And my earliest encounter with Jimmy Dean in the privacy of my own imagination as a teenager in Australia. I leafed through the plane's journals to pass the time and came upon a story in *Time* magazine about the presidential election campaign which was enveloping America during my visit. There in print was the comment from John McCain that his 'gaydar' gave him the uncanny capacity to know gay soldiers when he met them in Vietnam. If you already know them, asked the *Time* journalist, why is it necessary that they should not tell?

And then my eyes fell upon a story about George W. Bush— then the front runner for the Republican nomination. Don't expect an invitation for yourself and your partner if you are gay and Bush gets into the White House, the report warned. 'Don't ask, don't tell' will be writ large in the heavens of Washington. As my jet rushed across the Pacific, I thought about the progress, limited as it sometimes was, that we had made in Australia, and about the long way still to go in the United States. I also thought about the dusty answer I had given to a journalist from the university newspaper about the original reason for my commitment to human rights. I talked of our struggles in Australia for Aboriginal rights and for women's equality. I mentioned gay and lesbian rights, but I passed over the subject quickly. My personal story was, I thought, of no special interest to Americans. Why should I force it on them. It might embarrass my hosts. I should show good manners.

On my return to my office I sent an email to the university newspaper. It said:

> There is one thing that I failed to say during our interview and I regret it. I would like you to add to my answer to your question about the reasons for my response to non-discrimination. When I was growing up in Australia I learned that I was gay. I was told by everyone that I should be thoroughly ashamed of myself and of my feelings. I never accepted this. And as I grew older I became determined to do what I could to ensure that this was changed. That is why I asked to see the Students' Society OUT at Indiana University and to give its members encouragement and support. In Australia things are changing. Even in the United States things will change.

Things will only change if people speak up. They will only change if the game of shame and the spell of silence are broken.

The Quakers have always been the least homophobic of all major religious groups. They are simply 'Friends'. Not for them the denunciations of others about things they did not choose and cannot change. Having suffered discrimination, the Quakers do not dish it out. It proved to be a comfortable religion for Jimmy Dean. With lessons for us all.

- 4 -

JOHAN—
LESSONS IN LOVE

ACCORDING TO A BIOGRAPHY of Groucho Marx, the maestro's funniest moments occurred on a quiz show that lasted for fifteen years. There he repeatedly demonstrated his mastery of the snappy reply:

> Woman contestant: 'I've been married for thirty-one years to the same man'.

> Groucho: 'If he's been married for thirty-one years, he's not the same man'.

Reading this exchange on a plane somewhere over America I laughed aloud as I searched for recollections of the moment, then thirty-one years earlier, when I first met Johan. Little did either of us realise where that the chance encounter of a few minutes would lead and how long its story would unfold.

In Sydney in the 1960s, there were not many places for gay men to meet. At least there were not many if you were disinclined to run the gauntlet of police entrapment and other horrors in public facilities. Like many of that era, which for me is still symbolised by Police Commissioner Colin Delaney and his crusade against gay men, I concluded that love and companionship were going to be out of reach. This was long before gay liberation struck Australia. A lifetime's instruction in shame and denial took their toll on most homosexuals of that era, as, I suppose, it did on me. I entered a phase of silence and denial. Encounters, love and pleasure were consigned to a fantasy world. In the privacy of a room with a shut door, even Commissioner Delaney and his cohorts could not invade my secret imagination. But the real world, inhabited by real lovers and sweating bodies, was an elusive thing. Like most gays of that time, I thought of myself as a member of a tiny fractional minority doomed forever to travel in a world of silence and loneliness—a kind of *Flying Dutchman* of love.

℘

No one should underestimate the power of the human desire for love and companionship gifted by the sexual urge. One can intellectually embrace an idea of celibacy as the path that society seemed irrationally to enforce on people like me. But in the midst of the loneliness, the nagging demands of the body and mind, the heart would urge the spirit to look for what the law, religion and society forbade.

As chance would have it, in 1966 I was regularly acting as a pro bono attorney for the New South Wales Council for Civil Liberties. This was a group of earnest citizens who took it upon themselves to protest against governmental oppression in all its

forms and to defend its victims. Much of my voluntary work at
that time involved conscientious objectors who protested against
the call-up to service in the Vietnam War. Many days were
occupied in the cases that grew out of that conflict. They involved
mass arrests in Sydney of demonstrators protesting outside the
United States Consulate-General against a war which was sucking
Australia into its morass.

In the midst of these cases, and others that came my way
from Civil Liberties, one unusual matter landed on my desk.
It was out of line with the usual cases. And so was the client
who went by the name of Richard Graham. He was a young
New Zealander who was rather attractive both to look at and
in his somewhat flamboyant attitude to life. I later discovered
that Graham was not his real name but actually his first given
name. I have a dim recollection that he told me he came from a
'distinguished' family in New Zealand, of which he was a much
lamented black sheep. He had left a rural life in New Zealand
to make his fame and fortune in Sydney. His means of doing
this was to publish a journal called *Censor* and later a magazine
named *Obscenity*. These represented a deliberate challenge to the
prudish censorship laws of Australia in the early 1960s. Copies
of these rather tame publications can probably still be found by
those who really want them, deposited in the State Library in
Sydney and in the court files connected with the case involving
Richard Graham. My recollection is that they looked rather
similar to the student newspaper *Honi Soit* published by the
Students' Council at Sydney University. Cheap paper and rather
puerile and trivial contents with a lot of adolescent humour. But
also thrown in were extracts from *Fanny Hill,* an erotic novel
of 18th century England, banned in Commissioner Delaney's
Australia of those days.

Graham's publications were regarded by police as a frightful affront to public order and the decency of right-thinking citizens. He was nabbed, but not before police had solemnly secured an oral admission from him that he was 'editor, publisher and distributor' of the publication *Censor*. Graham and a hapless newsagent who had sold copies of the magazine *Obscenity* were prosecuted and convicted in Sydney's Central Court of Petty Sessions of an offence against the obscenity laws. They were fined $20 which, all things considered, was not a particularly cruel or unusual punishment in those days, or ever. Perhaps the magistrate was trying to show his own contempt for the bringing of such a prosecution.

The Council for Civil Liberties, however, was up in arms. It authorised the firm of solicitors for whom I then worked to bring an appeal to the New South Wales Court of Appeal to have the convictions quashed on legal grounds. That Court, in which not twenty years later I was myself to preside, upheld our legal objection. The police then appealed to the High Court of Australia. The appeal came on for hearing in Sydney just a few days after I was admitted to the Bar in July 1967. The report of the case shows that I appeared as the third and most junior of a team of barristers representing Graham and his co-defendants. It was my first appearance in the High Court, clad in my new robes of black cotton and wearing an all too obviously virginal horsehair wig. Our side lost the appeal. My companions at the Bar table were Jim Staples and Ken Horler. Chief Justice Barwick dissented. But the majority restored Graham's conviction and sentence. Little did I think that thirty years later, in Barwick's great building in Canberra, I would myself be occupying a seat on that Court. Life has a charming unpredictability.

Richard Graham was mortified at our loss. His greatest fear was that he might be returned to New Zealand, to the bosom of his respectable family, snatched from the wild life he enjoyed so much in Kings Cross. That district was not yet afflicted by drugs or much violent crime. Graham said that he was very grateful to me for my efforts on his part. As my reward, he took me to dinner. In the warm ambience of the restaurant, inquisitively he sought out the secrets of my loneliness. Once revealed, a great smile came across his handsome face. For him, although not gay, opening for me the door to the pleasures of the flesh became something of a moral challenge. He mentioned a friend who lived in a tall apartment block nearby whom he knew to be gay. This friend occupied a respected place in the entertainment industry in Sydney. A meeting was arranged. Into the luxurious apartment we strode. Richard Graham declared: 'Michael has a problem. He's like you. And he doesn't know how to go about finding a friend.'

The intermediary studied me with care. Having decided that I was not for him, he mentioned two places where I could meet a prospective companion. One was at a dance hall on Parramatta Road, Petersham, where a large party was organised every Saturday night. The other was The Rex, a hotel just around the corner, near the El Alamein fountain in Kings Cross. Both of these venues have since fallen to developers' dreams: the Petersham Dance Hall is now a social security office; the old Rex has been pulled down. Where the crowded bars of The Rex once stood, now an antiseptic apartment block defiantly claims its place. But in the Sydney of the 1960s and 1970s, gay men knew both these places well. Today, we remember them with nostalgia and affection. Here was a little enclave which, it seemed, Delaney's police left alone. At their doors the limit of the law's oppression was drawn in the footpath.

Armed with this advice, and with appropriate application, I set about the search for love. Richard Graham went his way. He is probably now a captain of industry in Dunedin. Quite possibly knighted. My venue adviser later climbed up further rungs on the ladder of respectability in the television industry. Two decades later, and out of the blue, I saw him sitting in the back of the courtroom in the Court of Appeal, just to see me at work in my theatre. After the case, I called him in to my judicial chambers. He was very well preserved for the passing of two decades. Cosmetic surgery, I speculated. Having done their work, Richard Graham and his friend dropped out of my life. But a door was opened. The world of loneliness would disappear. Not before time, one might add, for I was in my twenty-ninth year.

∽

For those who had not previously trodden this path (and for some who have), the entry into an unfamiliar world of places like The Rex and the Petersham Dance Hall was a somewhat intimidating affair. I do not doubt that it is the same for singles venues of every kind all over the world today. Pride, discretion, prudence and reserve, whilst admirable human qualities in other circumstances, are terrible afflictions in such places. The fear of a slight or, worse still, of outright rejection will sometimes make even the bravest hearts hold back from the manoeuvres that are essential to turn the occasion into something beyond drinking to stupefaction and staring into space.

The Rex in those days had two bars which, for a decade or so, were virtually exclusive to the gay community. The front bar, abutting the footpath in Macleay Street, was known affectionately (and not too subtly) as the Bottoms Up Bar. Behind it, separated by a bank of urinous toilets, was a slightly more luxurious back bar. It was less heavily populated at most times. Clientele marginally older. Music and lighting gentler on the clientele's ageing faces. There was a constant traffic between the two bars. Some visitors just looked around and did not even bother to stop for a drink, rushing out with a frown to signify their annoyance that their precious time had been wasted once again.

One Saturday night in late July 1968 I summoned up the courage to speak with a group of drinkers against the rear wall of the back bar. One of them was a young man who told me that he was a soldier. He confided in me his apprehension about being sent to fight in Vietnam. I could understand why. He suggested that I should come with him and his companions to the Petersham Dance Hall. I had never been there. I agreed. We climbed into a small car that made its way to Petersham, a suburb seven kilometres away. The hall in that inner western suburb, in the midst of an area then with many Italian migrants, was not far from Fort Street Boys' High School on Taverners' Hill, where I had received my secondary schooling. No alcohol was sold on the Dance Hall premises. It was necessary to buy drinks from a nearby bottleshop. *Cinzano* seemed to be the compulsory beverage of choice. And so I bought a bottle.

I went through my desultory and inexpert paces of dancing to the tunes played by a bearded band. Many of the songs of those days represented the familiar melodies of the Beatles, then all the rage. 'Hey Jude' was a good excuse for the lucky ones to dance cheek to cheek.

Then, out of the corner of my eye, I spied a truly beautiful man of Iberian appearance. He was dancing nearby, seemingly on his own, lost in thought. The soldier and his friends were forgotten. I began dancing with this mysterious Latin. He likewise abandoned his friends. Soon after, I remember accompanying him across the Sydney Harbour Bridge in a taxi towards my apartment at Kirribilli. I could not believe my fortune. He was twenty-four, with classic Spanish beauty. He told me his name was Demo. But Demo had been a bit too familiar with *Cinzano* that evening.

At Kirribilli, I just let Demo sleep it off. He was totally unimpressed by the spectacular views from my windows: of the Opera House, then being built, and the twinkling lights of the ferries on the harbour. All that Demo wanted that mid-winter night was to sleep. I sat looking at him as he slept. I feared that his beauty would slip through my fingers.

In the morning, after breakfast, I gave him my telephone number suspecting that I would never see him again. In fact, he called. The dream became a reality. Demo was my first love.

In December 1968 Demo agreed to come with me to New Zealand. I went to a travel agent, Mrs Boermeister. She booked the air tickets and accommodation. 'Does your friend need a visa?', she asked. 'Yes,' I said. 'What is his passport?' 'Spanish,' I said. So she did the necessary. We toured the north and the south islands together. I will always love that country. It was, for me, a special time. But just before the return to Sydney in late January 1969, Demo announced that he intended to continue his travels. As soon as we were back in Sydney, he was going to pack up and set out for Melbourne. I could not believe that the dream would so quickly evaporate. Like many before and since, I cried and protested. But I was to learn that you cannot demand love. It cannot be required no matter how much you give it or want it. It has to be freely given.

On 28 January 1969 I accompanied Demo in a taxi to Central Railway Station. He embraced me and boarded the train, struggling with his large suitcases. His Sydney adventure was over. A

Melbourne adventure was about to begin. He waved happily from his seat in the railway carriage. Opposite him, I noticed, was a young man equally handsome. The train pulled out. I went back to the apartment at Kirribilli. I shut the door. Alone again. Silent.

The Opera House was still being built. The little lights of the ferries were still crossing the harbour. Out there in the twinkling suburbs were thousands and thousands of people. Many of them, I knew, were lonely like me. Where would I find another Demo? I understood, of course, that there was no alternative but to resume the search at The Rex and the Petersham Dance Hall. Returning to a life of celibacy seemed doubly unnatural now. Demo, four years younger, had taught me what I instinctively knew. Humaneness is not naturally a solitary thing. I had in my mind the image of my own family with its feelings of love and wholeness of being in affectionate companionship. Solitude has its blessings. But not for long.

❧

'You didn't continue mourning for very long', Demo was to say to me years later. 'Just two weeks of mourning. Not enough!'

I am sure that Demo did not want my mourning to go on indefinitely after his departure. At least, I don't think so. But it did seem fitting to him that the young Sydney barrister with the nice apartment should miss him for more than two weeks. But that was the time that elapsed before I met Johan.

Why precisely I went out to The Rex on Tuesday 11 February 1969, I cannot now tell. Perhaps it was the mesmerising effect of the lights of that dazzling area known as 'the Cross' and the place from which I had set out to meet my first love. I had had good luck once. True, a relationship of seven months was not particularly long. Not long enough. But I also knew that sitting at home watching the television, listening to Bach's cantatas and feeling sorry for myself would get me nowhere. So on that night of chance I dressed in what I thought were suitably informal clothes. I set out for Kings Cross by ferry and a long walk. Before me lay, once again, the frightening challenges of the Bottoms Up Bar, with the smoke and the music and the lights.

As I entered the bar I recognised some of the usual suspects. A number of truly ancient characters—probably in their forties— were drinking a seemingly endless series of schooners of beer. I could never keep up with them. My Protestant upbringing had left me with incurable alcoholic inhibitions. But no-one seemed to care. This was a pretty tolerant place. 'Live and let live, I say' was the theme on everyone's lips. We all hoped that Commissioner Delaney and his men were in a good mood. The loud voices were in hopeless competition with the noisy piped music and its primal beat. Boom, boom boom, said the drums, in time with the beat of my heart.

I looked for quiet place in a corner from which I could survey the whole scene. I did not want to get engaged in conversation. Actually, I felt very sorry for myself. I was enjoying the feeling. I was sure—in fact certain—that there was no chance of finding another beauty like Demo. Having savoured the best, I was preparing myself for a life of premature loneliness, nursing the memory of my seven months of love.

I took a middy of beer. That would portray a suitable image, I thought—contemptuous isolation begging to be broken. I stood near one of the benches just inside the door that opened from Macleay Street. Suddenly I saw a new man, a handsome man. He was beautiful in a different way. In the place of the dark eyes and long eyelashes, black hair and restless body of Demo was someone of fair skin, blue eyes and high cheekbones striking a calm, almost serene, posture. Does lightning truly strike twice, I thought to myself?

We both remember the first words I spoke when, at last, I summoned up the courage to make an opening gambit. Since that moment of chance, we have both speculated on what our lives would have been if we had not gone to the Rex Hotel that evening. What would have happened if I had walked with a frown through to the back bar with its more subtle lighting? Perhaps in search of the abandoned soldier. Proximity drew us together. Fate intervened. Everyone who has had a companion of decades remembers how it all began.

'Who in this motley crew do you fancy?' I asked.

Johan swung around and turned his blue eyes on me. Until then, I gathered, a bit crestfallen, I had not even entered into his sights.

'Who in this motley crew do you like?' I repeated the question.

As I waited, I thought he was about to say, 'Well, certainly not you'. If he had, that would have been that. Long years of life together would have disappeared like a shooting balloon, expelling all the air of possibilities in a sudden deflation and the thrill of a clever put-down.

Instead, he turned the question on me. Good manners prevented me from saying, 'Well, actually, I rather like you'.

I heard from his accent that he was a foreigner. He looked the same age as Demo, about twenty-four, I thought. Hearing his accent, I guessed that he might have been a German. That excited me even more. I had studied German at school. Everyone told me that my German accent was good. No, it was superb—almost native. 'You have a *Sprachtsgefühl*', my teacher used to say. So I thought I might try out my language skill on this man. Not many

Australians could do that. If he were German it would truly be a point of fascination, I thought. I was already in overdrive. My mind raced ahead at all the possibilities. At the very least, I thought to myself, I might improve my German vocabulary with this man.

The words bubbling over to fill in the space, I asked this silent man: 'You sound like a German. I have just been reading a biography of von Ribbentrop. What do you think of von Ribbentrop?'

I must admit that, even if this unknown man had been a German, this was not a very sensitive question to ask. What an opening gambit. So gauche. So inappropriate. But to ask such a question of a Dutchman was bordering on the insane. I could see his blue eyes searching through the haze of cigarette smoke. Later, he was to tell me that it was at that point he decided the man standing before him was probably mad. Mad as a hatter. Talking about von Ribbentrop in a gay bar! What next? 'Get me out of here' was written all over his face.

This was only the second time that Johan had been to the Bottoms Up Bar. The first time, a week before, had been futile. He had been there for no more than an hour. No one in the motley crew that night looked at all interesting. Now the first person to speak to him was apparently deranged, babbling on about recent German tyrants. Moreover, as he tells it, my clothing looked extremely odd.

Clothing has never been a big interest for me. I had donned a pair of cream trousers and a sweater for my foray to the Rex. The trousers were of corduroy. The sweater, a thick orange one, was a trifle unsuited to the near heatwave conditions of mid-February in Sydney. The combination of the intense stare, the bizarre conversation and the inappropriate clothing in the airless bar almost led to a polite 'excuse me'. But Johan, like me, was lonely. He had never had a lover or companion. So he did not walk off. He was also well read. By the sheerest chance he was actually quite interested in history—even German history. He possibly knew more about von Ribbentrop than anybody in that bar that night. In such an unpromising way a lifelong love affair began.

We both drank another middy of beer. Neither of us wanted it to stop. When the bar closed at 11 o'clock, Johan suggested a coffee shop nearby. We left the Rex together. We walked past the fountain, all aspray. When we got to the coffee shop, we found that the business had changed. I observed that he knew as little about Kings Cross as I did.

'Why don't you come home to my place? It's just across the Bridge. It won't take too long to get there. I will make sure you get home,' I said.

We climbed into a taxi. We can both remember that the driver was also from the Netherlands. He seemed intrigued with what his two passengers had in common. He kept looking at us in his rear-vision mirror. Over the Cahill Expressway we rode. Over the Bridge that I had crossed eight months earlier with Demo. As Johan now tells it, when he saw the unit on the very tip of Kirribilli, with its spectacular outlook of the city of Sydney and its harbour, he thought, 'This is a man with real potential in the field of property'. As I was to discover, Johan had much greater interest than I about clothing, real estate and much else besides. We spent a good hour looking out of every window at the beautiful views. We watched together the sparkling lights and the little ferries plying their way across the harbour. He helped me move another single bed into my front bedroom. My mother, assuming a life of solitude for her eldest son, had helped me to furnish the apartment with single beds. But from midnight on

11 February 1969 a makeshift double bed was put in place. Johan van Vloten had entered my life. Not a day since that fateful encounter have we been parted in spirit. Lightning strikes twice.

༄

Johan was actually the same age as I. He was born a little more than a month after I was. He was twenty-nine, a fateful age, when we met. He came into the world on the opposite side of the planet. His birth fell on Sunday 23 April 1939, St George's Day. With names taken from his maternal grandmother, Johan Anton van Vloten's born in the Hague, was to be the last of the three children of Willem Nicholaas van Vloten and Bertha Aria Rietvelt. His father was a builder, skilled in a particular form of roofing work popular in Holland before the war. His mother, in between raising children, worked as a cleaner in the big homes of the rich and the hotels of the towns in which the family lived.

Johan's birth came at a dangerous time in Europe. Hitler's armies had swept into Czechoslovakia a month earlier. A new European War seemed imminent. His parents had lived through the First World War during which the Netherlands had remained neutral and was not occupied. Most people of their age expected war and knew in their hearts it would be different this time. As war clouds came closer Johan's mother began to prepare. Prudently, she spent all of her spare money purchasing soap. Palmolive soap. The collection of soap would become the precious currency by which she staved off her children's hunger when the invasion came and the occupation of the Netherlands followed in May 1940.

Johan's father, like many young men in Holland at the time, was rounded up and sent by the German occupying forces to France. There he was commandeered to help build the Atlantic

Wall. For years the little family grew up without their father. He was part of the slave labour of the German occupation forces.

As a child Johan was a delicate boy. The fear and stresses of the time took their toll. He was often hospitalised and frequently given to bouts of St Vitus' Dance, a nervous affliction manifested by constant rocking and movement of the head and face.

Fearful that the Germans and the Allies would bomb the towns on the coast, in mid-1940 Johan's mother gathered up her small brood and moved with them, inland, to Nijmegen a city on the Rhine to which the Germans assigned them. Even today Johan can remember the bombs and queues for food, the German soldiers and the fears and dangers of the war. His mother continued to exchange her precious collection of soap for scarce vegetables sold by farmers on the black market. Johan was pushed in a pram, a little blanket covering the boy and a few precious turnips as well. Beside the pram were his brother Frits and his sister Barbara, walking with their mother through the German lines and checkpoints. The names of the children, including Johan's, struck a resonance with the German soldiers. These were Teutonic names. They patted the children's heads and directed the woman with the pram to pass. They did not know what a canny operator in survival Johan's mother was. It was an instinct that he was to inherit.

Nijmegen was on the right side of the Allied advance into Holland which came to a halt at Arnhem late in 1944. Johan and his family were liberated by Canadian soldiers. He still remembers them handing out gifts of chocolate and sweets to the starving Dutch children. He remembers that one of these gifts, peanut butter, was shared with the family cat, which had somehow survived the war on the few precious left-overs the family kept from their meagre meals. The sudden intake of such rich food proved too much for the unfortunate cat. It had survived the bombing, but Canadian peanut butter carried it off. Cats have always been precious companions to Johan. He treats them with loving-kindness—better than some people treat their children.

At war's end Johan's father walked all the way from Normandy back to his family in Holland. His homecoming is still remembered. The little family was reunited. Life for them resumed a certain normalcy. But these were hard years in the Netherlands—years of poverty, food rationing and great floods that broke the dykes and swept flood water through the country. The first time Johan saw an orange was in 1947. He was eight years old.

The young Johan van Vloten was a studious boy who liked his books. He responded well to teachers, like Mr Klaasens who inspired him with tales of history and politics. He read as much as he could of the events of the world, fascinations beckoned by his lively intelligence. He still remembers his feeling of outrage on reading in *Panorama,* a Dutch weekly magazine, of the refusal of the British mandate authorities to allow a boatload Jewish refugees to reach Palestine. In the Avenue of the Righteous in Jerusalem, there are more trees planted to honour the sombre people of the Netherlands who hid Jews during the Occupation than any other land apart from Poland. On the basis of population, the Netherlands and its people stood against the oppression more than most. This was the land in which Johan grew up and from which he acquired his values.

Johan's family did not expect their youngest boy to pursue an education. Later, he was to gently criticise his parents for not encouraging him in his studies. But who can be too critical of people who had just survived the deadly horrors of such a war? At fifteen Johan began work in a factory outside Dordrecht, a southern city. It was owned by Dupont Chemicals. But he yearned to see the world. He badgered his mother to let him join the Netherlands merchant marine, which was at that time one of the biggest in the world. It boasted passenger ships of the Holland America Line and big cargo ships that plied the seven seas. This, he decided, is what he wanted to do. He gave his mother no peace until she finally relented. Going to sea was a part of the imagination of many generations of boys growing up in the Netherlands, a land itself rescued from the sea.

Johan van Vloten was engaged as a junior seaman. He was given his *Monsterboekje*, a sort of seaman's passport. He still has it. From time to time he has threatened to run off to sea again. In his *Monsterboekje* I can see the photograph of the handsome young boy whose greatest desire was to explore the world. He has often told me of the crashing seas and the fearful storms in the North Atlantic. To this day, I listen open-eyed at these descriptions. The worst seas I have known are those of Sydney Harbour when you get a hint of the Pacific Ocean as you cross the Heads. In the North Atlantic and Southern Oceans, the ships creak and groan in response to the anger of nature.

To his great annoyance and embarrassment, Johan's mother would come along in the early days to inspect the ships to make sure that they were sufficiently seaworthy to carry her son. The best companion of many a mariner was a bottle, but Johan has told me of the books that were his friends. Long periods of loneliness at sea were broken for some by whorehouses and intoxication. But Johan was gay. These outlets were of no interest to him. Instead, in port, he looked around for presents for his family. He handed over his pay to his mother. Life had settled into a predictable routine. With a meagre allowance, the young mariner brought encyclopaedias and other books which he kept in his home. He had no lovers. Contrary to the usual image, his life as a sailor was almost wholly sexless.

∽

In 1963, Johan made a fateful decision, to migrate to Australia. As with many emigrants, his first choice was the United States, but the quota from the Netherlands had been filled that year. He did not contemplate Canada. It was too cold. Instead, Australia increasingly beckoned. He had seen newsreels. He had read journals about the Great South Land. He abandoned his life in the merchant marine and chanced his fortune in Australia.

He left the Netherlands on a KLM flight organised by the Australian Embassy in The Hague. He was twenty-four years of age. At Sydney airport signs directed the new arrivals into buses leaving immediately for a migrant camp. The young single ex-sailor had not come all this way to settle down to routine in a migrant camp. Instead, he collected his meagre luggage and took a taxi into the city. He spent his first night in Australia in a hotel. By chance, he fell into conversation with another Dutchman who had work as a carpenter and shopfitter. This was not something that the young Johan had ever previously attempted but, in the manner of those times, within a day of his arrival he was fully employed. Astonishingly, he proved an accomplished carpenter. Soon he was sending money home to Holland, to his parents.

Johan's words of praise about Australia must have fallen on fertile ground. When he wrote to urge the family to join him in Sydney, he received a reply telling him that they had already booked their passage. He met their ship at Circular Quay with a large car he had just bought. He drove them to the house he had rented in leafy Dulwich Hill. Within a day, his father also had a job. He was later to work in a city building where he was provided with sleeping quarters that doubled up for Johan. This was where Johan was sleeping when he set out for the Rex Hotel on that night in February 1969 when our lives came together. Johan never went back to that city room.

✺

When I met Johan, he was working on machine tools in the Repco factory in North Sydney. He was embarrassed by this fact and the smell of oil that sprayed onto his body in the course of his work. For my own part, I found the smell attractive. Coming home from my life as a lawyer, I would find Johan soaking in the bath at Kirribilli trying desperately to get rid of the odour. Like most people from the Netherlands he was obsessively clean.

A few weeks after we met I received a phone call out of the blue from Melbourne. It was Demo. He invited me to join him in Melbourne for a weekend. 'Only one can take me away from you', I said to Johan. The look of hurt in his eyes was my reproach. But he was still there on my return. For many years afterwards, he would remind me of this event. The two men were totally different. Demo was a party-goer who loved dancing, music and the gay scene. Johan was organised, self-conscious, serious, a reader with no time for the scene. In the years that followed, we would ceremonially revisit the Bottoms Up Bar together on the second Tuesday of February to remind ourselves of the huge element that luck plays in life. Other than that, and an occasional sortie to the Petersham Dance Hall, we kept mostly to ourselves.

In July 1969 we decided to visit Fiji in the mid-year Law Vacation. I went back to the travel agent, Mrs Boermeister, to book the tickets. I remember her fixing me with her eye and saying, 'Spanish passport, of course?' 'No,' I answered colouring. 'Netherlands passport.' She could not suppress the raising of an eyebrow. They are not so far apart, I thought to myself, Holland and Spain. As Johan was to explain to me, the Netherlands had been ruled by Spain for a hundred years. And Netherlands still remember the intolerance of the period of Spanish occupation. From time to time, I thought he saw Demo in his imaginings as a kind of Spanish grandee, trying to intrude into the territory of the plain folks of the Netherlands, like him. In fact they met later years and got on well—mostly by describing to each other my unbearable faults.

So it was that as Neil Armstrong was making his giant leap for mankind on the moon, Johan and I were on a beach off Rakiraki in Fiji. We were joined to civilisation only by the flash of a mirror that would bring a boat when we were ready to travel to the mainland. It was there that Johan proposed we should make a great journey overland. He suggested we should acquire a stationwagon to sleep in and drive from India to England. He had read about an overland rally from London to Bombay at that time. The adventure appealed to his still unsatisfied desire to explore exotic places. At first I thought the idea crazy. But later I was to warm to it. It was the ultimate revenge of the mariner. To cover the great central landmass of the world by land.

We were to undertake the overland journey twice. The first adventure began in December 1969, not twelve months after we had met. It lasted a year. All my colleagues at the Bar warned me that it would destroy my legal practice, if not civilisation as we knew it. The second time we crossed the world was 1973 to 1974. Two years of travelling in a Kombi van. Lots of books of history, poetry, music and politics. Johan would tell me of the books he was reading, a course that he has followed all of our lives together. He was practical, interesting and wise. At this time he also developed a facility for learning English poetry by heart. Other things that interested him he committed to memory. In the quiet of a night under a starry sky in Goa or in the frightening mountains of Afghanistan and Turkey, he would suddenly burst into a sonnet of Shakespeare, or for the sake of variety, according to his humour, Abraham Lincoln's Gettysburg Address. I always found it astonishing that a man with no formal education beyond his fifteenth year had such gifts and interests. Lincoln's powerful words in a deep voice, uttered with a distinctive accent, is almost certain to bring on tears.

Back home we returned to our new apartment in Darling Point. Soon afterwards, in November 1974, he was with me when I told my family the news that I had been offered a judicial appointment. By this time, indeed within a couple of weeks of our meeting, Johan was fully integrated into my family. Every week he would come with me to visit my parents at home in Concord. My father was later to tell me how Johan's advent on the scene had signalled what he had long feared, that his first-born son was homosexual. With this realisation he wept and prayed. But his biggest fear was that my mother would find out. Homosexual people know that this discovery, often painfully realised, has also frequently heaped undeserved shame on parents and families. This becomes part of their own oppression as well. Yet with the arrival of a child's partner, fear is usually replaced by knowledge. Shame by love. Tears by understanding. That is the way that most families work. It is what happened to Johan, my family and me.

With Johan, my parents, my brothers and sister we talked earnestly about the judicial offer. I was very young for such a role, only thirty-five. But then the dye was cast. I was welcomed to the Arbitration Commission in December 1974. Johan, by now working for the Australian Broadcasting Commission, discreetly stayed away. In fact, he came to none of my judicial welcomes until February 1996 when I was sworn to the office of a Justice of the High Court of Australia. Even then, he was not named by me, or anyone.

Within weeks of my judicial welcome, I was appointed to a different post, Chairman of the Law Reform Comission. It was to take me away from the bench for a decade. In the Commission, the inquisitive media frequently asked about the private life of this young judge who was now leading this high profile body. Never did I volunteer the details of my private world. By the same token, I never denied it. I never descended to pretence. Not for me the close female friend to act as a 'walker' at public functions. Johan and I simply kept our private life to ourselves. 'I have appropriate domestic arrangements', a *Sydney Morning Herlad* profile in 1976 recorded me as saying. They were certainly 'appropriate' to us. They were no business of others.

In part, I suppose, we adopted this course because in those years it was expected that everyone in public life would play the game of shame. Laws against homosexuals, although still in place, were by the 1970s not enforced in Sydney against consenting adults in private. The fact that they were not enforced was often cited as a reason for delaying or denying law reform. Just leave well alone, those bigots used to say. Commissioner Delaney had departed, but the attitudes of his day were still alive in many quarters in Australia of the 1970s, even in the law.

Every Christmas I would invite the members and staff of the Law Reform Commission to come to the home in Rose Bay that Johan had created after 1976. In the manner of the Dutch, he would work furiously to have everything flawlessly spic and span. Then he would disappear. He did not return until he telephoned to make sure that the last guests had departed. I imagine that most colleagues and many friends of those years guessed about, or heard rumours of, the mysterious Dutchman. But my personal life was forbidden territory. We all knew the rules. Don't ask. Don't tell.

∾

In the years that we have been together, my family have come to know Johan's sterling qualities. Where we are sometimes up in the clouds with theories and ideas, he is distinctly down to earth. He is practical. He is well organised and always thinking ahead. After leaving the Australian Broadcasting Commission—where he became the Commission's paymaster, mastering with ease the arrival of new computer accounting—Johan went into a business partnership with a Dutch friend and his wife. They opened a newsagency in a northern suburb of Sydney. For three years I would sleepily become aware that he was leaving home in the dead of night to deliver newspapers. Reliable and punctual, he never missed a shift. They later sold the business at a profit. His nose for property has proved remarkable. If I had let him have his head, he would have moved house every couple of years. That is what his mother did in Holland when he was a boy. That, he explained to me, is the way people grow seriously rich in Australia.

In newspaper stories about him Johan is often described as a 'retired newsagent'. We smile because this description conjures up an image of a minor capitalist, dressed in a cardigan, perhaps wearing one of Patrick White's tea cosies. Nothing could be further from the truth. He is as much at home talking of his years on the high seas, reciting by heart a poem of Wordsworth, explaining a long forgotten point of medieval history, or singing a song in his deep baritone voice and in his mother tongue. He is a truly remarkable companion. Fortunate is a human being, straight or gay, who has such lifelong love. Evil are those who would deny such love to a fellow human being. God does not smile on such people.

∽

On Johan's sixtieth birthday in 1999, he and I were invited to a dinner at Government House, Canberra, given by the then Administrator of the Commonwealth, General Michael Jeffrey and Mrs Jeffrey. Deputing for the Governor-General, who was at Gallipoli for Anzac Day, the Governor of Western Australia, a war hero and soldier through and through, winner of the Military Cross in Vietnam, invited Johan by name to accompany me to the dinner. General Jeffrey and his wife were not to know that this was a special evening for us. When we arrived, the House was filled with generals and their wives. They had gathered in Canberra for the Anzac Day ceremonies.

Dressed in their striking red service uniforms and covered with medals, the generals out-dazzled Johan and me in our sombre black dinner suits. But looking across the table as he was deep in conversation with a general's wife, I allowed myself a momentary feeling of pleasure that it had come to this. That the man I had met at the Rex so long ago, who had given a lifetime to me, was being acknowledged as a person, as a citizen. The generals and their ladies took it all in their stride. Johan's dinner companion could not believe that he was sixty. She stroked the smooth skin of his face and asked for his secret. His blue eyes and high cheekbones still have the capacity to charm those who are willing.

I strained my ears to listen to their conversation. For a moment I thought I heard the name of von Ribbentrop fall from his lips. Surely not. With Johan on our journeys overland I have walked around the promontory at Gallipoli. We have ventured to the top of Cape Hellas. We have looked down to the Dardenelles. We have seen together the Hellespont where Xerxes took the Persian soldiers safely across on their way to Greece. We have walked to the beach of Anzac Cove. We have stumbled around the battlefields of France where much Australian blood was spilt. Johan would have more than enough to engage the generals and their ladies. And so it proved.

Since then, Johan has gone to many big functions. It is wonderful to behold the way he handles them all with civilised aplomb. Hidden away for a quarter of a century was this accomplished, intelligent, interesting companion of my life. Now, he is coming into his own. But not quite. For years, he enjoyed no protections under the Judges' Pensions Act. A wife of a single day could receive a full partner's pension. So would a husband. So would a de facto spouse of the opposite sex. But not for Johan of nearly four decades. During the long government of John Howard, righting that wrong was not on the agenda. The Attorney-General told me that in 1997. His successor repeated the statement in 2007 just before the federal election. Fortunately, Kevin Rudd took a different view. Coming to office as Prime Minister in August 2007, he moved with great speed. And strangely enough, when the proposed law was introduced into the Federal Parliament, there were virtually no votes cast against it. Where did the controversy come from? Where did it disappear to? Disappear it did. But other inequalities baffingly remain.

∽

From London in 1999, I telephoned Johan to ask, 'Would you marry me?' I was attending a conference on same-sex relations and the law. Like a good number of gay men in Australia, marriage, as such, has never been a high priority for us. Practical things, like pension rights and property protection appeared rather more pressing. But at the London conference I listened to lawyers from the United States as they explained the efforts, in that country (and others), to secure full constitutional and legal equality for homosexual citizens. The proponents of this idea accepted that the churches, synagogues and mosques were entitled, if they wished, to keep weddings in their temples to relationships between a man and a woman for life. But in so far as the state assigns to such a relationship civil rights and legal obligations, the speakers, one after another, argued that the state has no business to discriminate on the grounds of a citizen's sexuality. Where equal justice under law is proclaimed as an ideal, it is for the law to ensure equal rights to all citizens. Such rights should be available in a non-discriminating way to all who are prepared to accept the rights and obligations of a legal marriage, recognised by the law. Why are they denied?

As I listened to these arguments, I could see their logic. They required a distinction to be made that I had not much thought about between weddings and marriages and the assurance that the latter is available to all citizens. Hence the call from the public phone box in London to Sydney and my question: 'Would you marry me, if this were possible?'

'Are you drunk?' Johan replied. 'What are you doing over there? I hope this is a serious conference? Don't waste my time with such stupid questions. We can't even get the judges' pension'. The vision of metaphorically kneeling and proposing marriage was banished with disdain. Above all, Johan is practical. He has a healthy scepticism and a lifelong contempt for futile gestures and hopeless pipedreams.

The slow process of reform in relationship recognition has been a persistent feature of successive governments, Coalition and Labor, in Australia over the past decade. Whilst so many countries have leapt ahead to 'open up' marriage to same-sex couples, Australian governments have refused even to contemplate civil union or civil partnership. Even Spain and Portugal and Argentina have same-sex marriage. But in Australia we've banned civil unions and civil partnerships. This is a humiliating and outrageous denial of civic equality. According recognition in matters of pensions, money and material things is good and fitting. But denying equality in a matter that concerns the dignity and respect due to precious long-term relationships is hurtful, and against society's interest. Money is not enough. Dignity, recognition and acceptance are precious in their own right.

~

It was a long journey to and from the function on the outskirts of Sydney. I had started work at six in the morning in order to snatch a few hours from a busy time. At four in the afternoon I had set out in the car from the law courts in Phillip Street to give my lecture. This I did at six o'clock. The questions came thick and fast. By eight o'clock we were done and it was dark. After the reception drinks that followed I accompanied my hosts to a local club. The kitchen had just closed. 'Dinner's off,' said the chef. The cream cakes did not look appetising, so I declined them. My stomach protested the lack of food since lunchtime. The conversation and the questions from the bright-eyed participants ambled on. I reflected on the perils of public speaking in Australia. To these, it seemed, was now to be added starvation.

At 10 o'clock I rose and politely made my farewells. One of my hosts drove me back to town. Patiently, he explained all the problems that his life and work involved. I offered consoling words and well-meant advice. Three-quarters of an hour before midnight I was deposited at my home. The lights were out. Johan and the over-pampered cats Habash and Sheba were sleeping soundly.

On the noise of my arrival—and the lights—the three of them woke up. They were all staring balefully at me, the interloper. When I told my tale of woe, Johan began preparing some soup and toast. We sat down together. We talked in monosyllables about the events of the day. I polished off the meal. He still seemed half asleep. The cats looked deeply resentful of this interruption to their slumbers.

I suppose that a life of celibacy would have its own rewards. Returning to a dark home of silence and takeaway meals would probably be quite adequate in many circumstances. A solitary meal would certainly allow the events of the day, the month, the year or life generally to be explored quietly and alone, in the crevices of the mind. Perhaps a cat or a dog could look up before returning to sleep, indifferent to the clattering of the homecomer, deep at night.

But for most human beings that is not enough. It was not enough for me. It is not enough for most gays and lesbians as the agony columns of their newspapers reveal. 'Straight acting, good sense of humour, looking for non-scene person to age 40. Non-smoker. No drugs. Please answer. All letters replied to.' Column after printed column conveys this message. Not just for gays. For straight people too. And now they appeal to each other in cyberspace or on the ever-present iPhone. Beyond the dance parties and the Mardi Gras, homosexual people are human souls searching for love and companionship. Searching for the true friend. Hoping against hope for someone who will welcome their return home and offer words and actions that immediately translate love into reality. A bowl of soup, perhaps.

It is this hope that took the young lawyer and the young ex-mariner to the bright lights of the city. This is the flame that beckoned. It outshone the shame, the silence, the fear. It called the wanderer out of loneliness to the never ending quest for love.

RIVERVIEW—
A MODERN MORALITY TALE

THE LETTER WAS COMPLETELY UNEXPECTED. It was from a boy who said he was writing for the 'Hot Potato Club' at St Ignatius' College, known as Riverview, in Sydney. I recognised his surname. I had met his father years before when he was associated with a human rights organisation. The father was a fine man and a true upholder of human dignity. I held the father in high respect. It would be difficult to refuse the request of the son.

The letter invited me to come to the college as a guest speaker. As an inducement, I was told that I would be following in the footsteps of the Liberal Party's John Howard and Tony Abbott, and other notables. The topic suggested for me was 'judicial activism'. I explained that this was a subject that tended to excite politicians. The merest mention of it had sometimes led to attacks on the judges and the courts. So I was not prepared to talk on that theme. But I suggested, as an alternative, the subject of homophobia. I asked whether this would be 'too hot' a hot potato for Riverview? I urged my correspondent to check it out with the masters. I pointed out that the masters were bound to teach the official doctrine of the Roman Catholic Church. This teaches the 'intrinsic evil' of homosexual conduct. My message to the school would be somewhat different.

A little later I received a telephone call. The student asked whether I would be willing to accept a topic of 'social justice'. Now, speaking at schools was not something that I have regarded as part of my usual repertoire. I hardly had time to visit my own school, Fort Street High in Sydney, when it celebrated its sesqui-centenary in the previous year. Still, the young man sounded keen to have me speak. So I agreed to the broader theme to provide a context for my remarks. But I made it clear that I intended to talk, in that context, about homophobia. It seemed to me that this might just be the kind of topic that the masters of the school could not address themselves but which they might be happy to have an outsider talk about, from an informed point of view. The date was fixed.

Riverview is a Catholic school. It has a fine educational tradition. Founded by the Jesuits in the 1860s, it sits on a rise overlooking a magnificent natural setting, a tree-filled headland jutting into the Parramatta River which traverses Sydney. The site is priceless. The name by which the School is known is well chosen. I had often looked at it as I flew over the campus on the approach to Sydney airport. But I had never visited the school. So this would be a new experience.

I requested details about the school's famous old boys. The list came. I studied the names of the duxes and captains, the Rhodes scholars and the University Prize winners. I saw the name of Christopher Flynn in the list. He had topped the State in 1955, my year of the Leaving Certificate. He was a brilliant student, gifted in every way.

Shortly before the appointed day in February 2000, I received a fax about the engagement. I assumed that the sender was a student. After receiving my response, he replied to tick me off and tell me that he was a master. I apologised contritely for my error. However, I took the opportunity of the exchange to send him an advance copy of the text of my talk. I told him that I would not be reading it but speaking on the themes recorded there. I wanted there to be no mistake about the message I was bringing. Jesting, I expressed the hope that he would not be stripped of his laurels after I had given my address. He sent back another fax with the message 'fingers crossed'. I warmed to this teacher.

As chance would have it, on the day before my lecture the Roman Catholic Archbishop of Sydney, Cardinal Edward Clancy, issued a statement condemning the Gay and Lesbian Mardi Gras held in Sydney every March. He said that the Church recognised that there may be no responsibility on the part of homosexuals for their 'homosexual condition'. But he went on to say that the Church 'teaches that homosexual practices are contrary to the moral law' so that homosexual people 'are required to exercise self-discipline and avoid such conduct'. They are, he believed, called to a life without sex. The Anglican archbishop was contacted by the media and he endorsed the cardinal's statement. The two archbishops wholeheartedly agreed with each other that the Mardi Gras was a horrible spectacle of eroticism that promoted a homosexual 'lifestyle'. They called upon their respective flocks to stay well away.

The newspaper carrying this story pointed out that the Gay and Lesbian Mardi Gras had been operating for two decades in Sydney cheered on by hundreds of thousands of people every year. These two major Christian denominations had not previously ventured such an attack. In the past, castigation had generally been left to the Reverend Fred Nile, a Christian minister turned politician. He had been rewarded with the title 'morals campaigner' which invariably preceded his name in news reports. He was usually reported as praying for rain on the parade. Over the decades Mr Nile had mellowed a little in his attitude to the gay and lesbian community. Its members tended to treat him as the public figure they most loved to hate. They occasionally lampoon him in effigy and he has seemed in recent years to have taken it all in good grace. The newspapers therefore speculated as to why the big churches had taken so long to denounce the parade and why they had come out now. So far as the Catholic Church was concerned, 'pressure from Rome' was the guess of one religious correspondent. Whatever the motives were, the timing of the release could not have made the topic of my lecture more relevant.

∽

The white car drove me along the tree-lined road to the stone building that was the original edifice of St Ignatius' College. I was a little early. But three boys were waiting there. They were dressed in khaki uniforms. One, it turned out, was my correspondent. Since receiving the invitation I had unexpectedly met the father on a plane from Canberra. I told him of my intended theme. He expressed delight. Our conversation led to talk of youth suicide. If you bottled up a secret in your teenage years, one that concerned the very essence of your being, it was little wonder that occasionally the tension became unbearable. Australia had at the time one of the highest rates of suicide amongst young males in the world. Some of these, at least, could probably be laid at the door of shame, silence and homophobia. We agreed that an address at Riverview about sexuality, at the opening of a new millennium, could be timely.

The boys led me towards a classroom where they said the master was giving a lecture on Josef Stalin. As we walked across the school grounds through the Australian eucalypts, I could see in the distance glimpses of the city of Sydney and the harbour estuaries which proclaim for all to see that this was a school of tradition, wealth and exclusiveness. Many outsiders think of Roman Catholic schools in Australia as overcrowded versions of public schools. So it can sometimes be in the less affluent suburbs. But here, at Riverview, was Australian Catholicism triumphant, a school mainly for the sons of Catholics who have made good and who have turned to the Jesuits to give their children the best education that the Church can offer.

As I walked into class, the boys stood at their desks. It was a nice gesture, doubtless copied from the behaviour expected of them whenever a member of the religious community came into the class. In late years the numbers of that community have dwindled at Riverview. Photographs on a wall showed that, as recently as the 1960s, there were upwards of twenty-five of them. In 2000 the total number of Jesuits involved in the college was fewer than ten. Of those, two were men of great age. The laicisation of the college continued to gather pace. It was a familiar scene in Catholic institutions throughout Australia. On being told this, I asked the boys who were guiding me around if they thought Martin Luther would have the last laugh. Would they live to see married priests?

We strolled to the major buildings of the college. I asked to see the chapel. It was dark and rather small. It boasted a number of beautiful stained-glass windows. I asked the boys if the entire school community could still fit into its narrow confines. 'Only just,' they said. I noticed how the boys dipped their fingers in the water font to cross themselves as they entered this quiet space. They sat in the back pew. Their small gesture arrested me. It told of the differences which still marked off the Protestant from the Roman Catholic traditions of Christianity. For me there was no need of holy water. There was no sign of the cross. I went to the front and said my prayer:

May the words of our lips
And the meditations of our hearts
Be always acceptable unto you.
O Lord, our Mediator and Redeemer.

As we left the chapel the boys told me of how a retired master, now doubling as the college archivist, played the organ with gusto on Sundays and how much they all appreciated it. They were completely unselfconscious in the tour they provided for me. They took me to the depths of the old building. There I found quite a large area occupied by the college archives. In the midst of it was the archivist himself. Twenty years earlier, he reminded me, I had launched a book for him, on genealogy in Australia. We laughed together about the passing of time. The archivist complained that he was becoming rheumy.

On the walls were the photographs of old boys of Riverview from long ago—fading images of optimistic lads in the precious days of youth. The rowing team from the 1920s. Footballers from more recent times. Photographs of the college buildings over the decades. Pictures of gifted students like Christopher Flynn. Indifferent portraits of venerable, reverend gentlemen.

Even a photograph of clergy with the Queen. Honour blazers displayed in plastic covering which once were the preserve of the leading students but, in these more democratic times, were now available for many more.

The evidence of schoolboy pranks was there—cigarette boxes of brands long forgotten that reminded me of the postwar game of 'flickers'. I was interrogated about water bombs. Did they have them at my school? Dimly, I recalled a few of those missiles hurtling from the upper storeys of the more modest school building of Fort Street in the 1950s. There in the basement archives of Riverview were the carefully preserved memories of a wonderful educational institution. Here were the faces of boys who had passed through its gates, many of whom had gone on to become leaders of the Australian community. 'It is good that you keep all these records. I hope it will always be so,' I said to the archivist. 'Soon someone will have to take over from me,' he observed, with sadness I thought, as we parted and went our ways.

The boys took me upstairs to a richly decorated room where sandwiches were being offered for lunch. Should I wait for grace to be said, I asked? Grace, if it was said, was a private exercise. The schoolboys were already eating. My three guides were soon joined by other students, members of the Hot Potato Club. They let me know that it was rare for them to be invited into the inner sanctum where we now stood.

On the wall of our lunchroom was a smallish portrait of St Ignatius, patron of the college, and photographic reproductions of the portraits of Saint Ignatius' companions, including Saint Francis Xavier. Francis and Ignatius had travelled to a far region, a long way from their own land. They had found different people. I began looking at the extracts from the writings of these companions that were framed on the wall. They stood there as if attempting to capture the essence of the saintly message. One of the boys pointed me to the words attributed to Francis Xavier. The message was as simple as it was clear: 'But in the love of the Lord, we are all one'. It seemed to me a suitable text for my remarks to the boys. I scribbled it down. Coming from the companion to their college's saint, perhaps it would carry more effectively the essential message I was bringing. At the end of my talk I would read it to them.

∽

The appointed hour came. I was escorted to my place in the hall. The boys were streaming in. The master had warned me that 'university rules' were observed in the Hot Potato Club. The boys could walk in and out at their will. Their only limitation was that they could not bring food into the hall. I wondered if this was for the defence of the cleaners or to safeguard the speakers. But I need not have been concerned. Not a single boy left during my remarks. On the contrary, more and more came and crowded around the doors, peering in and listening attentively.

As I approached the speaker's rostrum, the boys again stood. These quiet courtesies are old-fashioned in the Australia of today. They are often missing in the young. My correspondent introduced me and I rose to speak.

It crossed my mind how, years earlier, almost fifty to be exact, a judge had come to Fort Street High to address the assembled boys in the school memorial hall. He was a famous old boy, Charles McLelland. At the time he was the Chief Judge in Equity of the Supreme Court of New South Wales. I had been introduced to him later and he had seemed to be a man of great age. He was probably as old as I was at Riverview. We too had risen for him. He had spoken to us very simply and directly. I cannot remember of what. But I can be certain that it was not the subject I was to venture for these boys. I hoped I would have that judge's gift of simplicity, to speak honestly and clearly.

Human beings are the intelligence of the universe. They are blessed with gifts of insight and moral judgment. This imposes on them uncomfortable obligations. Those obligations sometimes require plain speaking in the face of error, unkindness and injustice. So it has been in the past. So it will always be. If only somebody had spoken to me in the way I intended to speak to the Hot Potato Club. It would have gone straight to my heart. Perhaps things could be different now. But in a world governed by the Church's views of the moral law, perhaps they could not.

༺༻

I gave my talk. The audience was totally silent. I could see their intelligent faces playing on the words I uttered. When I first mentioned 'homophobia', three boys close to the front turned to each other and moved as if laugh, so unfamiliar was the word in that place. But for the most part there was silence. Seriousness. Was this respectful attention, like the standing in the class? Was it formal courtesy? Or was it a signal that the students knew that my message was important for them—a matter for their consideration as moral beings?

I praised the college, its famous and independent minded old boys and I lauded my own school. I told them that, just like students, churches have report cards that must be marked from time to time. In the matter of social justice, the churches came out on top for their concern for Australia's Aboriginal people, for the poor, for refugees and the sick and the dying. But the report card on the role permitted to women, on practical help to the drug-dependant and on sexuality showed a distinct need for improvement.

I referred to the archbishop's statement reported in the newspapers that day and gave my own point of view. The boys looked and listened quietly. I told them to have nothing to do with hate speech—'poofter', 'faggot'—or with gay bashing, bullying and harassment. I suggested that a life of celibacy was not a practical solution for homosexual people.

The very decline in the religious community at the college and beyond, I thought to myself, was a kind of proof that a life of celibacy nowadays was the life of choice of very few. I thought it might be impolite to mention this explicitly and so I did not. But those who condemn and demand silence in the years of youth must wear the moral burden of the family rejections, suicides and the despair that the world of shame and silence brings.

When I was done, the questions flowed. They were as acute as they were intelligent and independent-minded.

Did I believe that the cardinal had lost touch with the original role of the Catholic Church? I told the boys to respect their archbishop, as I did mine. Indeed, I told them that he commanded my affection as well as my respect. He was an important teacher. But on the matter of homosexuals' rights, there was a different point of view. It was their moral obligation to pay attention to what their bishop taught, but also to listen to what I said and to make a judgment for themselves. As I uttered these words I wondered if this was the viewpoint of someone brought up in the Protestant tradition. Was a Catholic boy free to reject the instruction of his bishop? Was he free to make his own moral choices on such a point?

Did I realise the Catholic Church taught that people should respect homosexuals and avoid discrimination against them, that it was only their sexual acts which were strictly forbidden, I was asked. I acknowledged that I was aware of this teaching. This is the teaching of 'love the sinner, hate the sin'. But I suggested that this was a rather unrealistic viewpoint. To demand a celibate life of countless millions of homosexual people, with different capacities and inclinations for a life of celibacy, was unrealistic, unreasonable and even unnatural for most of them. So the sin-and-sinner distinction was a false dichotomy. And if they were in any doubt, they had only to consider whether it would be reasonable to demand of themselves that they follow an entire lifetime completely without ultimate personal and sexual fulfilment. Such fulfilment was an aspect of being a whole human being. To call on gays and lesbians to 'show discipline', in the sense of denying absolutely the fulfilment of their deepest human feelings, was similar in some ways to trying to change a person who is left-handed.

I told the boys of how, back in the 1940s at North Strathfield Public School, a teacher had tried to force my brother Donald, who is left-handed, to change to right-handedness, so that he would write like all the other boys. Correct slope. No smudging of ink. My mother had gone up to the school and remonstrated with the teachers. She demanded that they should stop this attempt at once. They did. How proud I was of my mother for doing this. We need more parents to remonstrate against those who insist on attempting to change a person's true self. I suppose that there would be some who could be made to write with their non-dominant hand. However, for all but a very few it would be unnatural. It was wrong to try to force it upon them, just as it is wrong to force a different sexuality.

One boy asked if I would stand aside in a case before my court involving a homosexual person. I told him that it was everybody's right in a court of law to have a judge who was competent, independent and neutral. This was a right I respected and upheld. However, my colleague Justice Mary Gaudron would not disqualify herself simply because a person in a case before her was a woman or because an issue was raised that affected women's entitlements at law. Heterosexual judges would not disqualify themselves from sitting in a case involving a heterosexual rape. Judges of particular ethnicity or religion would not normally be obliged to disqualify themselves because a case involved a person of similar background.

Yet there were limits I told the boys. Before my appointment to the High Court, I had joined the Movement for the Ordination of Women in the Anglican Church. I had done this believing that the Church of Jesus made no distinction amongst its ministers on the grounds of gender. Unexpectedly, a case involving that issue had then come before the Court of Appeal of which I was then the president. I had disqualified myself. I had taken no part in the hearing. Accordingly, the case had to be decided by other judges, two of whom were Catholics and one a Jew.

Later still in the High Court, proceedings were commenced by Rodney Croome, a leader of the Tasmanian organisation for reform of the laws against gay people. Years before I had sent some money to this organisation when it had run out of funds because I supported its cause. I never thought that it could become an issue before my court. As things transpired, soon after my appointment to the High Court the case involving Mr Croome was listed for hearing. Unhesitantly, I stood aside. The moral of the story, I said, was probably that you should join nothing and certainly give no money to anybody. The boys laughed.

One young man towards the front rose. What business was it of the Church to dictate what people did in the privacy of their own bedrooms, he asked. This was a brave and strong question. I felt he had understood the message I had brought. But I reminded him that the Church had a right to express its views, although he should consider them and ask whether the Church was wrong on a particular point, as it sometimes had been in the past. Equally, it was entirely proper for churches to instruct their congregations to avoid cruelty and unkindness to others, in bedrooms or anywhere else. Certainly, there was the need in sexual matters to teach of the duty to respect other human beings, to protect the young and the mentally incompetent, and to uphold human dignity. But the Church's doctrine was that the only place for sex was in the heterosexual marriage bed. This left nowhere for gay and lesbian people to go. Yet in the enormity of space, with all the planets, the stars and the galaxies, this minor variation in the sexuality of a comparatively small proportion of human beings should have been no big deal. A moral rule was needed that would acknowledge their existence and their human needs. Eventually the churches would realise this.

One student asked if I had felt a heavy burden lift when I publicly acknowledged my homosexuality. Fleetingly, the old hymn that I had sung as a schoolboy when the discoveries of life were upon me came into my mind:

> By the cross, by the cross
> Where I first saw the light
> And the burden of my soul rolled away.

I told this questioner that in recent years I had not felt burdened at all. I had lived to that time for thirty years with my partner, Johan. My sexuality was known to my parents, my family, my neighbours and most of my friends. It would have been pretty hard to keep such matters secret in a place like Sydney, in a country like Australia. Governments of all political persuasions had known of my sexual orientation. They had still appointed me to various offices, I hoped on my merits. But I acknowledged that if I had been as open then as I was now about being homosexual I would probably not have been appointed to the High Court of Australia. This was the reality of the world we lived in. It must be changed. Prejudice against people on the grounds of their sexuality often prevented them from reaching their full potential. This was why many people still played the game of shame and kept silent. Yet to demand silence was to impose undeserved shame. The spell could only be ended if people were honest and open. I had a moral duty to be so. Others may not be so free. Everyone must make their own choices. My hope was to make it a little easier for those who came later than it had been in my early years.

The questions rolled on. But my time was nearly up. By now a large crowd had gathered around the doors. It was clear that more boys were coming forward to listen. A vote of thanks was expressed. It was followed by prolonged applause. I was presented with a Riverview tie. Once again the boys stood. I walked out into the sunshine.

∽

'You had a big crowd,' said a master. Another pointed out that I had been competing with the college diving competition. 'I think you won,' he said.

We walked to the front of the school. There a plaster cast of Jesus of the Sacred Heart stood in the garden. Again an element of our religions that divided us, for that vision of Jesus had no place in the Protestant tradition of Christianity. The boys told me in shocked tones of how a car had recently dragged the statue over and broken it in pieces. 'In pieces like a potter's vessel' I thought, and Handel's *Messiah* came swimming into my mind. The statue had already been repaired. It stood restored, white and pure, in front of the old building.

'When my son was at this school he perpetrated an original prank,' said the master with a smile. 'He painted white footsteps from the statue to the swimming pool and back.' In earlier times, I thought, this might have been considered evidence of a miracle: 'Jesus walks in our midst. He is always with us.' You might expect that a master's son would think up the best student misbehaviour.

As I left the college the master handed me two papers. One was an extract from the *Catechism of the Roman Catholic Church*. Homosexual people, it declared, were called to a life of sexual abstinence. The other text was 'Meditation on the love of teaching' that he had written. 'I have heard that you are interested in teaching. You might find this worth reading.' I thanked him. 'I owe so much to my teachers,' I said. 'I only wish I had said so more often and to them.'

Later I opened the master's essay. It bore the hallmark of a fine teacher who realised the privilege he enjoyed of enlivening the young spirits entrusted to his care. Next to the priesthood, he wrote, teaching was the most important vocation. A prudently modest hierarchy, I thought, with which some might differ. Law was decidedly lower on the master's scale of virtuous vocations. But then a passage caught my eye. It contrasted two great university teachers of the 1930s. One, the distinguished

German philosopher Martin Heidegger, abandoned his Jewish friends in the Third Reich in order to win the prize of Rector of the University of Freiberg. The other, Pierre Bergson, Nobel laureate, was a Jew living his last days in Vichy France. In 1941, just weeks before his death during the Nazi Occupation, this famous professor of literature climbed out of his sick bed to go and register as a Jew, as the law required. He stood in line with other Jews. He acknowledged who he was. He rejected silence and hiding. According to the master's estimate, 'Bergson's teaching confirmed . . . that truth mattered and that it could be found'.

Clearly implicit was the instruction that we must all follow Bergson. Even if it involves difficulties and dangers, we should stand up for ourselves, as we are for who we are. We should stand before the world and with those who are, like ourselves, liable to discrimination and worse. We must reject the path of Heidegger. It is the path of truth that we must ultimately pursue not the path of worldly laurels. It is the truth that sets us free. Fortunate were the schoolboys of Riverview to have such a teacher.

࿇

The white car was there once again, waiting. Soon I was on my way back to work. The following day a newspaper declared that my message at the school had been 'It's okay to be gay'. Of course, this was not quite the message I had brought. To be accurate, the headline should have read 'It's okay if you're gay'. This was not a 'lifestyle'. This was not a fad to be turned on and off like a tap at whim.

The media tried to breathe passion and division into this rather low-key affair. But for the unexpected announcement by the archbishops, after twenty-two years of silence on the Mardi Gras, it might not have been noticed. My words to the boys would have remained with them. But no fewer than three reporters covered the story for the Saturday edition of *The Australian* two days later. They stated that there had been 'outrage' and 'uproar' at the school over my talk. There were even rumours that parents had come on Friday to take their boys out of the school. 'Rubbish,' said one of the masters. One student was quoted as expressing resentment at having to listen to my opinions with which he disagreed. Another boy reportedly said that the reaction amongst the boys had been 'overwhelmingly positive'. Other commentators were to rush into print in the ensuing week. Many letters were written to the editors of local and national newspapers. Many were published.

A letter by a parent to the *Sydney Morning Herald* referred to the high rates of suicide amongst boys in Australia. She expressed her support. 'God bless you Justice Kirby,' she wrote. Amen to that. But a spokesperson for the Council of Catholic School Parents told the *Sunday Telegraph* that I should apologise to the parents of the boys who had listened to my talk. Those parents knew, she said, that there were homosexuals 'out there'. But they sent their children to Catholic schools to get a particular moral instruction, not to hear the promotion of a forbidden 'lifestyle'.

Spokesmen for the Church were generally cautious in their remarks. True, one seemed to hint darkly that the Jesuits in charge of Riverview were responsible for all the unwanted trouble. But the headmaster issued a short statement saying that the school did not necessarily agree or disagree with the viewpoints expressed by visiting speakers. And through all this noise there were phone calls, faxes and emails—some full of hate but most of support, including a number from parents of boys at the school. One mother said that not only did she applaud what I had done for the college but that her son too had appreciated my talk.

∽

In quiet moments since my visit to Riverview I have returned in my mind to the privileged environment of that illustrious school. To the trees and the sandstone and the lively faces. Riverview College had, after all, gone ahead with the invitation although it knew my topic and the master had my text. This says something about the school's integrity and the primacy accorded in it to the boys. My theme did not prove too hot a potato for the Hot Potato Club. And perhaps out there in the mass of thoughtful faces, looking and listening, was a boy to whom I was speaking directly of issues secret and profound. If so, I have, in part, repaid my debt to the silent days of my own youth. That boy is no longer alone. And he deserves the love and support of his family. Of his community. Of his school. Of his teachers. And, above all, of the Church of Jesus.

- 6 -

OUT IN AFRICA—
OF JUDGES, AIDS AND TRUTH

*You can't expect us to agree to removing the criminal law
applicable to homosexuals. That might work in countries like
Australia. But it will not work here. This is Zambia. This is not
South Africa. Why, South Africa has even accepted homosexual
marriage. It is unacceptable in Zambia. I think it is good that
we came to this seminar. It exposes us to new ideas. But what
works elsewhere does not necessarily work in Zambia. We have
our own culture and beliefs.*

THE JUDGE WHO SAID this was sitting in a corner of a meeting
of Zambian judges called in 2007 to discuss the role of the law
in responding to HIV and AIDS. She was dressed simply and
exuded a business-like air. She folded her papers, pursed her lips
and looked down at the desk. No eye contact. She made it clear
that she did not approve of this talk of 'men who have sex with
men'. In fact, it offended her. She was angry. She was upset.
AIDS is like that. There will be a lot more anger and distress

before the epidemic in Zambia is brought under control. This outburst had come before I told the gathering of judicial brothers and sisters that I was gay. Was I just wasting my time there? Did the woman judge speak for all?

Earlier the same year, during similar meetings in India, I had discussed with the South African judge Edwin Cameron the invitation I had received to go to Lusaka. Tall and dignified, this proud and intelligent man, full of compassion and energy, is not only openly gay, he is also quite open about the fact that he is living with HIV. In his remarkable book *Witness to AIDS*, he emerges as one of very few Africans who is honest about the impact of the epidemic on their own lives. So what did this forthright South African judge advise about the trip to Zambia? His views were clear and quite definite.

'Oh, I did that a couple of years ago,' he said. 'Naturally, I told them that I was gay and HIV positive. The day after my visit, the local press screamed that the judges had been addressed by a gay judge. The Chief Justice was reported as saying that he wished I had not introduced that subject into my talk. So I gather it was not very welcome. Just the same, they later invited me to return to Zambia for another seminar. So they either forgot my "indiscretion" or they forgave me. Perhaps they came to see its relevance to the subject. Certainly, you should go there. They are facing a tremendous crisis with HIV. But they are very conservative, even by African standards. You have to expect a rocky road'.

Zambia, the former Northern Nigeria, is at the very epicentre of the most serious location of the HIV/AIDS epidemic. Over 1.6 million adults of sexual age are infected with HIV in a population of little more than ten million. This is a huge rate of infection. It shows a lack of leadership. It speaks of national complacency.

What could I tell an audience in Zambia that they would listen to and act upon?

∽

The invitation to visit Zambia was issued by the civil society organisation ZARAN (Zambian AIDSLaw Research Advocacy Network). Founded by law students at the beginning of the twenty-first century, members shared a belief that more needed to be done, including in the law, to confront the problems of ignorance, denial and discrimination that were impeding the response to the AIDS epidemic in their country. Eventually receiving some funding from foreign donors, the organisation set up an upstairs office in the main shopping street of downtown Lusaka. Some of the founding lawyers have remained involved in ZARAN, even after graduation, but most of those early enthusiasts drifted away, recruits to the commercial law firms. One lawyer for whom commercial law was not enough joined me at dinner after the judges' seminar.

He was a fit, small and wiry young man with a broad smile and a ready willingness to laugh at the foibles of his fellow Zambians. He apologised for missing most of my visit. 'My wife and I have just been blessed with the birth of our son,' he declared, and the widest smile of all brightened his face. I thanked him for his continued involvement with ZARAN. This was work for every mother's son, and for their daughters too.

He was keen to know the reaction of the judges to my talk. He had heard that I had told them I was gay and was all ears to know how they had reacted to this judicial outing.

He listed the gay friends he had made through his work with ZARAN. He talked warmly of Edwin Cameron and other mentors who had inspired his commitment to the struggle against the epidemic: 'I've no problem with homosexuality, myself. But the difficulty here is that we are still living in the past. Shame leads to silence. And in the face of AIDS, silence means death.'

∽

Travelling to Zambia to speak to a group of judges was not easy, given my timetable that month which already included a first meeting with the Lawyers Collective in Mumbai. As chance would have it, UNAIDS (the United Nations body responsible for leading the world in the struggle against the spread of HIV) had invited me to a meeting of its reference group on HIV and human rights which was to be held in Geneva between 12 and 14 February 2007. A window of opportunity opened up. I could take the night flight from London to Lusaka, on my way home to Australia, leaving me with little more than a day in Zambia. What could anyone achieve in such a short time?

Part of me hoped that this plan would not prove feasible. As I well knew, judges have their sitting schedules fixed weeks or months in advance, so maybe the meeting would not be possible given its short notice. Maybe I would be spared the risk of upsetting the Chief Justice and his colleagues with my talk about sex and gays and drugs and death from AIDS.

Yet something inside urged me on. A visit to Zambia would close the circle of trips to the old federation of the two Rhodesias and Nyasaland. In past years I have visited Zimbabwe, in happier times. On one of those visits I stayed at the Victoria Falls Hotel. Across the gorge and through the permanent mist and the rainbow produced by the mighty falls, I had seen Zambia in the distance. Every Zambian I met had assured me the falls were even larger and more beautiful on their side. A visit seemed enticing, yet there was no way I could travel the five hours by road to Livingstone to see Victoria Falls again. My encounter with Zambia would be confined to Lusaka, a modest and not especially attractive city with dusty streets and a few tall buildings. So what urged me on?

The thought of a country that objected to the merest mention of homosexuality alarmed me. The published figures concerning the Zambian epidemic showed that 8.5 per cent of the HIV infections involved men who have sex with men (MSM). One United Nations official at my meeting in Geneva was to caution me: 'Don't worry about them. The locals don't. Basically they don't care about such people. They are perfectly willing to write off MSMs, the CSUs [commercial sex workers] and IDUs [injecting drug users]. These are just immoral people. Basically, if they have HIV or AIDS, it is a punishment from God for their immorality. They deserve it for their sins. Writing such people off comes naturally to those who regard such people as only temporarily separated from Hell's fire.'

∽

In Geneva, I called on Peter Piot, then the long-time Executive Director of UNAIDS, a fine scientist and epidemiologist who had led the organisation from the time it was set up in 1995. Most officers of the United Nations can only serve in their posts for a maximum of two five-year terms as this is the limit that applies to the Secretary-General himself. But Peter Piot was an exception. He had been carrying the burden of leading UNAIDS for more than a decade.

As a young scientist from Belgium, Piot had travelled in the 1970s to the former Belgian Congo. He played a leading role in identifying the ebola virus. Not content with this significant scientific achievement, he turned his considerable intelligence to a new condition, sometimes called the 'slim' disease that was then emerging in the Republic of Zaire, now again named Congo. Piot saw uncanny similarities between this new infection and the condition of GRID (Gay Related Immuno Deficiency) described by the American Centers for Disease Control in a cohort of gay men in Canada and the United States. Many scientists at the time ridiculed the supposed link between the two conditions. How could they be connected? The African condition was appearing in the general population. So what was the connection with the unusual condition described on the opposite side of the world amongst affluent, well-nourished males? Piot was untroubled by the criticism of his research. As we now know, he was right. Before long the link was universally accepted. The era of global HIV/AIDS had arrived.

To lead the energies of the World Health Organization, Director-General Halfdan Mahler initially chose another gifted epidemiologist who had also worked as a young doctor in Zaire, Jonathan Mann, to take the helm of the Global Program on AIDS. Peter Piot worked closely with him—at least until Mann dramatically fell out with Mahler's Japanese successor as WHO director-general, Hiroshi Nakajima.

When Mann was given orders to clear his desk another American, Professor Mike Merson of the Yale University of Medicine School, took charge for a short time. But then Peter Piot assumed the responsibility of leading the new inter-agency body created on the initiative of UN Secretary-General Boutros Boutros-Gahli. Piot proved to be an inspired choice. To lead the world in such an urgent, devastating struggle was to grasp a poisoned chalice. There was no vaccine to prevent infection with HIV. Nor was there any cure. Yet Piot accepted, as Jonathan Mann had taught, that the best hope of halting the spread of the epidemic lay, for the time being at least, in behaviour modification. How could medical science enlist the social sciences to stop, or at least diminish, the spread of the fateful virus? Everyone knew that the law was only ever partly successful in persuading people to modify their conduct—especially where that conduct was intensely pleasurable and important to personal identity. So how could law be invoked to support the efforts of scientists like Peter Piot to contain this deadly and unexpected disease, especially in Africa?

∽

Just short of sixty at the time of our Geneva meeting, and showing the stubble of a close cropped beard, Piot is a man who disdains formality. He normally appears tie-less and dresses in casual clothes, as he did when I joined the group of experts examining the ongoing human rights challenges of the epidemic. I knew that Piot had visited Zambia just a few months earlier, so asked for his advice for my talk with the judges and lawyers. What he told me was sobering. It reinforced what Edwin Cameron had told me.

'I saw the former president, Frederick Chiluba,' he said. 'I started to tell him of the urgent need to adopt legal changes to win the confidence and attention of those at the pointy end of the epidemic—sex workers, gays, drug users, people engaged in serial sexual intercourse. The president immediately reached for his Bible, which was close by. He told me that what I was saying was "against the Bible". Of course, I was raised a Catholic. So I knew all those biblical passages. I knew the arguments and the counter-arguments. But Chiluba would not be shifted. Perhaps the new president, Levy Patrick Mwanawasa, will be more enlightened.'

'You should just try to convince them. I encourage you to do your best,' he continued. 'Tell them the universal things. Stay on message. It is worthwhile. Some in your audience may pick up the points you are making. After all, judges are supposed to be amongst the intellectual leaders of countries like Zambia. When you have finished with Zambia, we can use you elsewhere. There is nothing unique about the Zambian resistance to the hard decisions that have to be made to tackle AIDS effectively. It's a very common problem'.

With these words about Zambia, Peter Piot and I drifted into recollections of the early days of AIDS. Of the charismatic Jonathan Mann, tragically killed in 1998 in an airplane disaster off the coast of Canada. Of Nakajima with his disdain for AIDS and human rights strategies and his fascination with trivial things such as commemorative postage stamps with an AIDS theme. Of Luc Montagnier and Robert Gallo, the scientists credited with identifying HIV, and their uneasy relationship in the initial meetings of the Global Commission on AIDS to which I had been appointed by Mann. Of the debt humanity owed to Halfdan Mahler and to successive directors-general of WHO following the end of Nakajima's reign.

As we talked of these personalities and the brilliant scientists whom Jonathan Mann gathered around him, I could see Peter Piot in my mind's eye at the early global conferences about HIV—a young man standing at the microphone, raising the unmentionable problems, asking the unanswerable questions.

He was still doing this some three decades later. But for some time he has also engaged his envoys to carry on the struggle in countries far from the antiseptic UNAIDS office building in Geneva. Peter Piot was to leave UNAIDS and a fine legacy in 2009. He went on to London's Imperial College for Science, Technology and Medicine, where he is now Director of Global Health. His successor, Michel Sidibé, is now the third great leader in the global struggle.

Before I left Geneva for Zambia, I met Staffan Hildebrand, another survivor from those early days of AIDS, and one of the brilliant cast that gathered around Jonathan Mann. Now a celebrated Swedish filmmaker, Hildebrand was in Geneva to produce a film to mark the twenty-fifth anniversary of the global campaign against AIDS. He spoke gently of the films he had taken of Jonathan Mann, and of Mann's sharp intelligence and clear vision. With the tape rolling he interviewed me. Was I optimistic about the struggle against HIV and AIDS? Yes, I said. The human species is genetically programmed to survive. If necessary, it would take bold steps to tame the spread of this disease, even steps that challenge basic intuition and enliven deep prejudices. Was this the right answer, I wondered. Other species have disappeared in time because they would not adapt. Yet humanity has unique capacities of consciousness, rationality and communication. Would these see us through? Would these human characteristics be my companions in Zambia? These questions were with me as I travelled south to Zambia.

∞

The plane descended to the African tundra through several layers of cloud. Delicately it lowered itself until the green of Africa was clearly visible. Zambia had enjoyed a plentiful rainfall during that year's rainy season. The maize crop, like the copper price, was up and promising. Yet, unemployment was terribly high. Many young people came down from up-country, searching for regular work but unable to find it. Desperate circumstances, ready-made for cheap sexual favours and the comfort of a warm body.

The plane's door opened to an inrush of heat. The weary passengers blinked in the sharp morning sunlight. In the airport hall, I walked towards a counter marked 'Diplomats and VIPs'. My letter of introduction from the judiciary, bidding me to give the keynote address at the seminar, seemed to impress the immigration officer. When I told him, in answer to his question, that I would only be in Zambia for little more than a day, he declared with a self-conscious flourish, 'I'll give you a visa for three days.' Armed with the stamp in my passport, I walked through the hall to the small group awaiting my arrival.

Carrying a sign with my name was a young man collecting just a little too much weight. He called himself Pablo. I remembered the name from the emails for it was a curious one, neither African nor British. Later I discovered his real name was Paul, but it seems he was obsessed with soccer and had renamed himself after a player whose fame had not yet impinged on my consciousness. Pablo was to be my guide over the next day and a quarter in Zambia. He was quiet and, as I was to discover, often just as conservative as the judges whose countryman he was.

'We have put the seminar back because the plane was late,' Pablo announced. I begged for the chance to take a shower, receiving the distinct impression that this would be all right only if I did not take too long about it. 'It wouldn't be a good look for me to make an appearance unshaved and unwashed.' Pablo, however, declared that my modest beard was hardly noticeable and that I should not worry on that account.

The car pulled into a luxury hotel on the outskirts of Lusaka. The shower revived me and I ventured down to the conference hall adjoining the hotel. In fact, I arrived just in time and was beckoned to stand in a small group assembled to await the Chief Justice's motorcade. 'The CJ is on his way', I was told with what looked like genuine excitement.

A few minutes later a convoy of cars swept into the hotel grounds stopping at a distance from our little reception party. We scurried off in the direction of the cars. I remembered the arrival of President Daniel arap Moi of Kenya at another African legal conference a few years earlier. His Rolls-Royce and escort vehicles showed then how well the British colonialists had taught their African subjects to aggrandise governmental office to command respect, fear, awe. The Chief Justice of Zambia had no Rolls-Royce. Indeed, each judge arrived in a four-wheel drive, and sat rather incongruously in the rear seat. But the convoy was impressive in its own way, surrounded as it was by soldiers in uniform. The Honourable Ernest Sakala, Chief Justice of Zambia, shook my hand warmly. I could see him puzzling about where we had met before. Later we were to discover that we had attended the same Commonwealth Law Conference in Melbourne a few years earlier. There he would have been a face in the crowd. However, in Lusaka, he was the star turn.

The women who greeted the Chief Justice did so with a little bob—rather like a curtsey. He asked one pretty woman her name and what her work was. He did not seem specially surprised to find that she held a senior post in his own court. In this republic, I gathered, the court did not mix, especially with the Chief Justice.

✎

Ushered out of the sunshine into a darkened hall, I sat with the Chief Justice and his deputy, David Lewanika. A fine young lawyer welcomed the Honourable Lordships on behalf of ZARAN. He proposed that the conference begin with the national anthem: an invocation to patriotism commonly practised in most of the developing world and observed less often in developed countries with their more low-key nationalism. As bidden, the whole assembly stood to sing Zambia's anthem. Strong, free and united is Zambia, they declared. I could imagine them at schools before Zambia gained independence in 1964, singing the old royal anthem which then passed as the song for Northern Rhodesia. Amidst the hopes and dreams of those days of freedom from colonial rule, no one would have imagined the new scourge of AIDS that would confront the young country and its people just twenty years later.

Their voices strained, the seminar participants sang the words as unenthusiastically, I thought, as Australians proclaim that their land is 'girt by sea' and has 'boundless plains to share'. The only other African national song I knew was the old Nigerian anthem I learnt as a young man participating in a delegation of Australian university students to that country:

Though tribe and tongue may differ
In brotherhood we stand
Nigerians all, and proud to serve
Our sovereign motherland.

By 1978 this song, with its stirring melody written by a British woman on the eve of Nigeria's independence in 1960, had been abandoned. The abortive attempt to establish the breakaway nation of Biafra had led the patriots of Nigeria to consider its anthemic references to differing 'tribe and tongue' as unhealthy in a country, and continent, riven by linguistic and ethnic divisions. The English, French, Belgian and Portuguese colonists might have ignored those differences in dividing the continent and setting their boundaries so unnaturally. But in that carve up, Zambia, with its six major ethnic groups and languages, was assigned to the British Empire. It was to prove a fateful assignment for it brought in its train the penal code that brought the common law's condemnation of 'unnatural sexual offences'.

I knew at once, as I looked around the darkened room, that were I to sit in court in Zambia, it would not take long to master the issues of fact and law and to feel at home. We had the same way of doing things, the same old-fashioned courtesies—'my learned friend', 'with respect', 'inter alia', and so forth. The robes and traditions were familiar. It was these common features of judicial life that would perhaps afford me a chance to reach into the minds of my audience and to engage them in the legal issues of the AIDS epidemic. Perhaps, because of our shared traditions, I might be able to persuade them of the role that the law could play in reducing the impact of HIV and of helping to contain its spread.

The anthem had at last come to its close. Zambia was proud and free and I was with a group of people who had special responsibilities to keep it so. We took our seats and I was surprised to see about fifty judges present. A good roll-up: the nine judges of the Supreme Court of Zambia, many judges of the High Court and of the Industrial Relations Court. All of them seemed rather reserved. I was certainly glad I had decided to wear a dark suit, white shirt and the tie of the Inner Temple in London which had recently appointed me an honorary bencher. This was definitely not the occasion for informality. Dark suits and white shirts ruled in this outpost of British traditions.

Two of the Supreme Court judges in attendance were women. Three of the Industrial Court judges were women. I felt a kindred relationship with the industrial judges. As I told one of them later over lunch, industrial relations was where I had begun my judicial journey back in 1975. She did not seem surprised. 'Yes, we have our feet on the ground. In the Industrial Relations Court we meet the ordinary people of Zambia. It helps us keep in touch.'

Another variation to the program was proposed, to curtail the briefing on the nature of HIV and the response that Zambian government was taking to the epidemic. Pablo and his colleagues were willing to assume that the judges knew the basics about AIDS. They wanted to make the most of my presence at this unprecedented encounter with the senior judges of their country. Here was the cream of Zambia's judiciary. We had to maximise the time.

Chief Justice Sakala was a large man with a pleasing informality that belied the protocol and deference that surrounded him all the time. As he rose beside me to give the opening address, a young official scurried up to him, in the manner of a viceroy of earlier times, and presented him with a written speech. While the substance of the speech was probably written for his approval by ZARAN itself, the Chief Justice candidly acknowledged the serious problem facing the Zambian people. Indeed, AIDS was described as a 'peril' threatening the extinction of mankind. It was time the Bench took major steps for the protection of human rights, the Chief Justice declared, so as to ensure Zambia's response to HIV was 'rights based' including in the courts.

The speech recounted the horrifying statistics for Zambia, with one in six adults living with the virus. This was an intense epidemic. Of the 1.6 million Zambians who were HIV positive, 350 000 were in need of antiretroviral therapy, yet only 35 000 were receiving these vital but expensive drugs. This had led the lead international funding agency to question where its money had gone and explained its decision to stop finding Zambia. Naturally, the Chief Justice did not dwell on this shocking statistic. He simply emphasised that HIV/AIDS was a major health emergency and to the burden of the virus had to be added stigma and shame.

The Chief Justice uttered all the right words, pushed all the correct buttons. He even eloquently declared that it was not governments that gave rights to the people. Human rights were not the gift of politicians or even the State, including judges. They belonged to the people themselves. They inhered in the human dignity of each individual. They belonged to Zambians as their basic human rights.

A good start, I thought. The language of inherent rights reflected the philosophy that all people were equal exemplified by the seventeenth-century's John Locke and the eighteenth-century's Jean-Jacques Rousseau. If such ideas had truly taken root in this poor country of Central Africa, there would indeed be hope that these judges might be open to the message I had come such a long way to deliver. However, my knowledge of how these speeches were sometimes written and of the gulf that often appeared between words and action, kept my feet perhaps too firmly on the ground. The voice was that of the Chief Justice. But were the words and thoughts really his? Did he truly believe what he had just read? Would his response to the problems that I would describe follow through on the fine language? Chief Justices are

sometimes politicians of their courts. Often, they cannot escape
having to work closely with ministers and governments in ways
that ordinary judges can escape. Occasionally, they take on the
features of political life. I would soon find out whether this was
true in Zambia, as in so many other places I knew.

❧

Two medical experts spoke. They outlined the features of HIV,
how it spread in the general population, and how it did not spread
(mosquito bites, toilet seats, kissing and hugging). The Zambian
epidemic and its contours were described. The worst levels of
the infection were in Lusaka and in the copper belt in the north
of the country, where there were high concentrations of single
males, many of them without work. Yet, overall, more women
were infected with HIV than men. As with the sweepers, whom
I had seen bent over, cleaning by hand the highways that led from
the airport, the burdens of AIDS fell mainly on women. Zambia
followed the familiar pattern of poor, developing countries.

'These are your daughters and sons. Your cousins and uncles,'
the medical experts declared. No segment of Zambian society
was free from HIV. Even the judiciary? I wondered. If one in
six adults was affected, it was likely that some of the learned
judges sitting at the table were also HIV positive. None would
declare that fact. I did not expect that a Zambian Edwin Cameron
would suddenly arise in our midst to say bravely, 'I am living
with HIV; I am positive'.

The scientific sessions concluded and we walked out of the
darkened room into the bright sunshine. I snatched a sand-
wich and wondered for a moment what time it was in faraway
Australia. I banished that thought for the hour of my address

was near. Time zones and lack of sleep must be forgotten. The energy of the moment must be captured for the purpose was a large one by any account.

I saw officers of ZARAN securing the signature of the judges to a schedule they were passing around. 'Are the judges paid an allowance for attending this seminar?' I asked. 'Yes. It's about $35. The Chief Justice gets a larger sum. The government has laid down the condition for seminars like this.' I thought that, if such modest payments of donor aid could secure such a large turnout, it was a small investment to make to potentially capture the minds of the judiciary and court officials to devote a day to the issues of AIDS. Would they have come without the payment? Were they present because of a real engagement with the issue? Were they in attendance because the Chief Justice had told them to come? Or were they fired up by the enormous suffering of their fellow citizens? I was willing to give my audience the benefit of the doubt.

I noticed that most of the judges had attached to their coat lapels the enamel badges with the red ribbon that has become the international symbol of the struggle against AIDS. I could not imagine that judges in my own country would accept such an insignia so readily, lest it compromise their appearance of complete impartiality. But there it was. A room full of red enamel ribbons. Those who did not wear the badge stood out. Perhaps, after all, this epidemic has bitten deeper into the Zambian population than I imagined. Maybe these judges have indeed had loved ones infected by HIV. Perhaps they are fearful for their families, their children, themselves. Maybe they will be more receptive than their reputations, dark suits and reserved behaviour had suggested.

The earlier speakers had addressed the seminar from their table or sat behind computers to offer PowerPoint slides to illustrate their remarks. For me, it was important to engage personally with this new audience. I wanted to speak directly to each and every one. What must they be thinking of this white foreigner, projected at short notice into their midst? The challenge was to find quickly some common ground and then to win their confidence.

∽

We were all judges together, I told them. We each knew the hard and unrelenting days of being on the bench. Time was important to us. So I skipped over my planned introduction and told them about myself.

As judicial colleagues, they nodded with appreciation when I told them of my visit to Nigeria, so many years before, in the days of youth. I described the special green of the vegetation of Africa, so striking to an Australian from the driest continent on earth. I described my role as the independent co-chair of the Constitutional Conference of Malawi in 1994. At that conference I brought together the ruling party and all the opposition groups of that country to reach agreement about constitutional amendments that would end the reign of Malawi's first president-for-life, Dr Hastings Banda. The agreement had avoided bloodshed and converted that poor malarial country adjoining Zambia into a vibrant democracy. Zambia had taken a similar move in 1990 when its first president, Kenneth Kaunda, had agreed to relinquish one-party control. The elections in 1991 in Zambia had had the same outcome as in Malawi: a change of government and a new president, Chiluba. I wanted them to know that I was not entirely a stranger to Central Africa. A part of my spirit would always remain in Malawi. Many of them nodded in appreciation.

The judges laughed when I told them that, of all public officials, we were the only ones who could be counted on to be on time and to do their own work. They concurred that we rarely got applause or appreciation and then clapped when I announced my recent ascent to the Everest of being the longest serving judicial officer in Australia. And again when I described how my predecessor, a distinguished woman judge appointed in 1974, had only retired after my threat to poison her coffee.

I felt I had established empathy with my audience, an empathy fashioned by history, shared service and ideas about law. The common law comprises a great global community. It remains behind when the governors and soldiers and the politicians depart. We were part of this system. We could learn from each other, even about the strange epidemic that was the immediate reason for our encounter.

I described the early experiences in Australian courts of the AIDS epidemic. I told of how the first defendants in Magistrates' Courts in Australia whose HIV status had become known, were brought into court by guards dressed in 'moon suits'. While this ignorance about the dangers of HIV quickly passed, it showed how we must be on our guard against similar ignorance, stretching into our own time. 'Do not respond to AIDS', I said, 'based on fear or prejudice or intuition or religion. Respond with knowledge based on science and accurate information.'

One by one, I told of the cases that had come before me in my judicial life affecting people living with HIV. In one case, in the Court of Criminal Appeal, the question was presented concerning the sentence passed on a prisoner who had been infected with HIV. Should his term of imprisonment be reduced, in recognition of the fact that his life was severely shortened, as it was in those days? Should it be reduced because the burdens of isolation in a special unit in prison would increase his suffering and possibly accelerate his deterioration and death? Or should it be increased because of the special horror of AIDS and the need for him to be particularly careful not to spread the contagion? What did the judges think about that puzzle?

Every day judges have to grapple with controversies over which good people can easily differ. Still, I was surprised by the generally hard-line most of those in my audience took when I asked their opinions. For them, HIV was not a reason for mitigating punishment. In their view, the rule of law required no differentiation whatever between the sentence of prisoners according to their HIV status.

I pressed them on this point. Sentencing is, after all, a judicial craft. It requires reflection both on the seriousness of the crime and any relevant features in the life and background of the prisoner. Why was the prisoner's health condition not relevant as a personal factor that effectively increased the burden of any term of imprisonment imposed? My persistence was unrewarded.

The Chief Justice cautioned about the need for care in expressing views on this subject as a case was in the pipeline to come before the courts of Zambia that might present the issue for judicial decision. I reassured the judges. We were only speaking of these issues in general and hypothetical terms. Every judge knows that the level of judicial decision lies in the detail of the case. How many of us have made a judgement and then seen it attacked in the tabloids? Typically, the media rarely reveals the crucial evidence that explains the reason for a decision. With this comment a ripple of applause broke out in the audience. Many of them, I inferred, had suffered from unfair media attacks that are now such a feature of judicial life everywhere.

I could see, from the discussion of the sentencing issue, that this was going to be a hard day. Perhaps the very extent of the spread of HIV into the adult population of Zambia made it difficult for them to conceive of any allowance for the imprisonment of a person living with HIV. I tried to imagine a Zambian prison. Were condoms available there? I will not go in that direction yet, I thought. So I spoke of the wise words of Chief Justice King in a South Australian case of *The Queen v. McDonald* (1988). King's thinking ran along lines similar to my own. HIV was not a licence to commit crimes with impunity. But it could, on occasion, be relevant to sentencing. This was now the general view adopted by courts in Australia. My Zambian colleagues appeared distinctly unimpressed.

I moved quickly to cases that I had heard in more recent years concerning the application of discrimination legislation in instances affecting people living with HIV. For the Zambian judges, some of these problems might arise under their constitutional Bill of Rights. For us in Australia, it arose under specific laws prohibiting unjustified discrimination on the basis of HIV status.

There was the case of a drop-in centre for HIV-positive people proposed for the city of Perth but denied planning approval by the local government body. Was that an impermissible denial of 'services', contrary to the Act? How would that notion of 'services' be interpreted in the context of an anti-discrimination law specifically applied to the activities of local government bodies? The judges seemed doubtful about the approach that I had favoured. More sympathetic was their reaction to a case involving a soldier who had been dismissed from the post of signals engineer in the Australian Defence Force when a post-recruitment test disclosed that he was HIV positive. Was his HIV status incompatible with 'the inherent requirements of' his position as a serving officer in the army? Was an ability to 'bleed safely' on the battlefield, truly an 'inherent requirement' of all contemporary military service? Or was his sudden discharge from the army a discriminatory act based on imputed characteristics of HIV without regard to their particular operation in the employment of this soldier?

The judges laughed when I described how one of the judicial opinions had quoted poets of old to paint a vivid picture of 'rivers of blood' on the battlefield. For the first time, it seemed, there was a glimmer of understanding that HIV required a new vigilance against stereotypes, rules and indifference to their impact in the particular facts of the case. A distinguished Indian judge had once declared that HIV did not permit employers to condemn those living with the condition to 'economic death'. The Zambian judges, it seemed, could agree with that view.

I switched tactics. One after another I described the leading cases in which judges had considered the impact of law on people living with HIV. In an Indian case, the dismissal of a labourer, who was otherwise quite healthy, was set aside as contrary to the rights provisions in the Indian Constitution. Likewise, a decision in South Africa had ordered reinstatement of an airline attendant dismissed when his positive test results were disclosed. The judges now appeared to understand the cases I was describing. Progress, at last, was indeed being made. But, like the peace of W.B. Yeats in the 'bee-loud glade', the progress came 'dropping slow'.

When questions and comments were called for, it was mainly the Chief Justice and his deputy who responded. This, I thought, was always a danger of a meeting with judges. The observance of deference and hierarchy is so ingrained in the judicial psyche that judges lower down the pole are commonly loathe to express their true opinions. This may be natural loyalty, or it could be a prudent course given that elevation in the judiciary might sometimes depend on the good opinion or otherwise the Chief Justice. Where approbation could secure promotion and disapproval could condemn a judge forever to serve in some far distant province, the temptation to silence might be overwhelming.

❧

The seminar was proving a hard slog. I wondered how I could make these judges more sensitive to the legal needs of people living with AIDS and more understanding of their plight. Why were there no cases from Zambia in the UNAIDS case books when there were cases from South Africa, Botswana and Lesotho, despite the epidemic in Zambia being already so intense?

At lunch I sat with the Chief Justice, who asked if he should say grace before our meal. In the midst of such a terrible epidemic, a reminder of our blessings could indeed be suitable. The Chief Justice crossed himself and rapidly intoned a familiar prayer. There was no mention of people living with HIV.

I asked the Chief Justice about the whereabouts of the Anglican Cathedral in Lusaka. Somewhat pointedly, he told me he could direct me to the Catholic cathedral. I realised that my inquiry would have to be made elsewhere. In outposts of the former British Empire, Anglican churches are often a depository of interesting memorials—of earlier perils and faithful stewards bringing the 'light' of their religion.

As I was to find, however, religion had become a real part of the problem in tackling the challenge of HIV/AIDS. In Zambia, and in other parts of Africa, the missionaries had drawn bright lines to distinguish the moral and from the immoral, especially in matters sexual. In the age of HIV, these lines often presented difficulties in reducing the isolation of those most at risk of infection.

By chance, the ZARAN seminar coincided with an important meeting of archbishops of the Anglican Communion, held in Dar es Salam, Tanzania. The meeting had been summoned to attempt a reconciliation between the Anglican leaders of Africa, led by Archbishop Akinola of Nigeria, and the American branch of the Episcopal Church, led for the first time by a woman—Archbishop Katharine Jefferts Schori—itself a grave provocation to some. The Americans had earlier recognised the consecration of Bishop V. Gene Robinson, a gay man living in New Hampshire with his same-sex partner. To Akinola, who often compared same-sex relations to intercourse with baboons, this was a satanic perversion of biblical authority. Completely unacceptable.

Observers were predicting schism in the Anglican Church, with the conservative African prelates leading their flocks away from the liberal error of the American Church. Only two voices in the African Church could be heard regularly calling for calm and Christian reconciliation. One belonged to Bishop Desmond Tutu, former leader of the Anglicans in South Africa and a hero of the long battle against apartheid. He urged his African brethren to re-order their priorities and to concentrate on the real issues of the Church in Africa—AIDS, hunger, orphans and poverty. The other preaching the same theme was Tutu's successor as archbishop, Archbishop Njongonkulu Ndungane. 'I am not here to fight the American battles,' he declared a few days before the Lusaka meeting. Ndungane promised to work behind the scenes to avoid a rift in the Church. But many of the African archbishops seemed bent on forcing the issue. Tutu declared that everyone seemed to 'need someone they can look down on'. For African archbishops, it appeared, gays fitted that bill perfectly. The demons and fears of accepted religion were waiting for me in our afternoon session.

❦

So now was the time to launch the most difficult message I had brought with me to Africa. This was about the paradox of AIDS. The most effective legal responses to the HIV epidemic involved reaching out to those infected with HIV, and those at risk of infection, and providing them with legal protections. By doing this for injecting drug users, men who have sex with men, commercial sex workers, prisoners and other disadvantaged groups, as well as vulnerable women, there is a chance that they will receive the message of self-protection. Without a vaccine and a cure, only self-protection can prevent the rapid spread of infections. Only by preventing individual infections will the cycle of community spread of HIV be slowed.

I described for my Zambian colleagues the measures that had been taken along these lines in Australia and other countries. I explained what was meant by the 'rights-based approach', a direction endorsed by the Chief Justice in his opening address. I instanced the fall in the growth of the epidemic in my own and other countries. I asked if Zambia would be willing and able to take the brave and strong steps necessary to make an effective dent in the epidemic. I told the judges that the level of infection in their country was completely unacceptable. Something was needed to break the cycle. But did Zambia have the will to grasp this painful challenge?

I should not have been shocked by the response that was to follow, but I was. One judge pointed out that people whose health had been restored by access to antiretroviral treatment still remained capable of infecting others. This had led him to think that perhaps it was best to save the money and not to treat such people once they became infected. Another judge recounted stories about infected people who had boasted of deliberately taking many others with them to death from AIDS. Several judges spoke of the supposed cures for HIV that had been found by experts in traditional African medicine, including the promise of relief from HIV by 'sleeping' with a virgin girl. I had heard all these stories before, years earlier in discussion of the epidemic with Indian judges.

Several seminar participants complained about Australia's own policies on HIV, especially as they affected Zambians. One judge reported that young people seeking student visas had been refused travel rights to Australia after being revealed as HIV positive. Surely this was a departure from the indivisibility of universal human rights, I was asked. Does Australia practise what you have come to Zambia to preach? Another judge told of a case he had handled when in the Zambian Office of the Attorney General, before his appointment to the Bench. A long-term resident of Zambia, who was an Australian, had been expelled together with his Zambian wife only to be forced to return to Lusaka by Australian authorities where he was imprisoned at the airport as a health risk. It was a sorry tale which, if accurately told, brought little credit on both countries. These messages were designed it seems as a riposte to my fine words.

I reminded the judges that I was not in Zambia as an apologist for the actions of my government, but that generally speaking, both at home and abroad, Australia had been fairly enlightened about HIV. My purpose was to see if any of the successful strategies we had adopted, including the law, would have relevance for Zambia.

It was then that the woman judge of the Industrial Relations Court responded. She was not going to be lectured by those who were urging acceptance of gays or sex workers or others who had engaged in 'immoral' conduct. There was more than a hint in her anger, and in the intervention of some of her colleagues, that immorality attracted its own punishments. The hardness of heart of the response shocked me. Was there no compassion for the sick? Were they not fellow citizens of a free country whose anthem about unity we had sung just a few hours earlier?

When a special condemnation was made of South Africa for enacting legislation to permit same-sex marriage after the decision of the Constitutional Court of that country, I felt the time had come for greater candour. To remain silent might have involved complicity in a false understanding which honesty required me to remove.

So I answered the woman judge with the downcast eyes and pursed lips. Africans, so long the subject of denigration and discrimination, had to understand that they were not the only ones who suffered pain from such behaviour. Different views might be held about same-sex marriage, but it was not a subject to be dismissed as self-evidently intolerable or diabolical. I was gay, homosexual, I told the seminar participants. I had the blessing of a relationship with my partner that had lasted, to that time, thirty-eight years. In fact, our anniversary had fallen during the journey that had brought me to Zambia. On the previous Sunday, from Geneva, I had telephoned Johan to thank him for his loving kindness over such a long time.

I told the judges that we had discussed the issue of marriage when it arose in the debates of the 1990s. But, after all that we had been through in our lives, it was not a priority for us. The refusal to permit this civil status to a small proportion of citizens who wanted it, undoubtedly had serious legal consequences for them. Did I detect a few judicial heads nodding at this turn of the dialogue? One thought that usually unites judges in a common bond is the injustice of their salary and pension entitlements.

Trying to explain the loving relationships that can occur outside heterosexual marriage, I recalled a television program broadcast shortly before I left Australia. It had shown a number of elderly couples. In each case, one of them was suffering from dementia, some with Alzheimer's disease. Although in many cases the affected spouse did not even recognise the other, the gentle fidelity and love demonstrated in the face of great adversity was a marvellous example of kindness, shining through the ordeal. I expressed no doubt that if I reached such a sad state, my partner would show the same loving care for me—as I would for him. Such love could not be wrong in moral terms. Certainly, it was in society's interests to promote and support it. Fidelity and companionship could be great blessings in any human life. I expressed the hope that judges, as decision-makers who based their conclusions on evidence and not prejudice, would always face such questions with open minds. I indicated my intention to visit the Cathedral in Lusaka that afternoon, to meditate on a peaceful outcome for the episcopal meeting in Dar es Salam.

The Chief Justice asked what I thought that outcome in my Church would be. I did not know. But I hoped it would be based on the principles of love and reconciliation that I understood to be at the heart of my religion.

If I were to go to the main street of Lusaka and declare that I was gay, The Chief Justice continued, I would be arrested. This was doubtful, I responded, because the criminal law was concerned with acts, not mere words. This was a rudimentary point, but it showed the measure of the feeling against gays present in the room. The words of the warning of Peter Piot came flooding back. In this country, to be gay was considered to be 'against the Bible'.

But HIV and AIDS was bigger by far than all of us. The statistics on the epidemic in Zambia showed that about 8 per cent of the HIV infections were attributed to men having sex with other men. Even if this figure was under-reported, the spread of the virus in this group was not, unlike Western countries, a major component of the epidemic. 'So let us return to the issues most pressing for the majority of the population,' I enjoined them. 'Let us put to one side for the moment the 8 per cent, without writing them off for they are human beings and citizens too. But let us concentrate on the 92 per cent and decide whether any of the strategies adopted elsewhere would work in Zambia.' There was great relief at this invitation.

Poverty lay at the heart of the Zambian epidemic, several of the speakers urged. No law could be enacted that would easily sweep that hated scourge away or help the women who became sex workers in desperate need of income for themselves and their children.

It was not for judges to change the criminal law or to alter the legal rules governing drug users, sex workers, prisoners or anyone else, I acknowledged. The challenge was for the judges to consider what could be done by them to bring the unacceptable levels of the epidemic down.

So had the level of infection declined as the Deputy Chief Justice claimed? The epidemic had indeed fallen a little. It may have plateaued, explained the local UNAIDS officer Dr Catherine Sozi, a tall, intelligent medical doctor from Uganda. But it was still much too high. She supported the 'rights-based approach'. Only when people were protected from discrimination and the fear of stigma would they to come forward, take the HIV test and observe behaviour that would prevent further spread of HIV. Hers was a telling intervention. It added a powerful message of the need for a rational and supportive approach on the part of the law. Punitive morality would only drive the epidemic further underground. It would reinforce discrimination in a land that had learned its sexual morality from uncompromising missionaries. A new approach represented a big ask.

∽

We broke for another cup of tea—always a welcome companion to the judicial life. The judges did not crowd around as usually happened at conferences. They were quiet now. Perhaps they were considering Dr Sozi's warning that they and their families would not be exempt from AIDS unless new and different responses were tried.

I would have done my Zambian colleagues no service had I skirted around the sensitive issues that we had discussed. Judges, by vocation, are not strangers to truth. Amongst themselves, they are constantly obliged to exhibit candour and share knowledge and true opinions. Whilst our views might have differed on some of the topics we had discussed, we would all be the wiser for the exchange.

In the closing session I invited Dr Sozi to join me at the top table. Without any provocation on my part, she said Zambians would be deceiving themselves if they thought there were no men who had sex with men in their country. Denial was not the path to follow in tackling HIV. Honesty was essential. And to honesty I added the need for a love for one another. I assured the judges that in the early days of the epidemic I had sat at the bedside of twelve good friends who died of AIDS. It was a cruel end. It imposed a moral obligation on us all to spread the word of prevention. And to demand the basic right to available treatment.

We all emerged from the meeting room and stood together in the afternoon light for a group photograph. A courteous exchange of farewells followed. And then the cavalcade of the morning was repeated in reverse. The chauffeured four-wheel drives picked up their judicial passengers. All in hierachical order. They swept away, as quickly as they had arrived, to their courthouses. I hope, like me, they reflected on the lessons of the day. At the very least they now had the books of cases I had left for the Supreme Court Library. When cases eventually come before them involving aspects of the epidemic affecting so many of Zambia's people, they would know where to look. If they turned south, particularly to the Constitutional Court of South Africa, they would find judicial guidance of great wisdom to support them in their decisions.

∽

As dusk rolled in, I asked Pablo and his colleagues to take me to the Anglican cathedral. They knew exactly where it was. The Cathedral of the Holy Cross was a massive building, constructed on the cusp of Zambia's independence under the loving leadership of Archbishop Oliver, the last European to hold that office. Absent were the colonial relics and the English-style stonework that often marked out such buildings. But in one corner, near the great door that Oliver must have commanded to open when the cathedral was consecrated, was a small chapel. Through coloured glass, I picked up the crimson colours of the Union Jack and the banners of the erstwhile Northern Rhodesia Regiment. With these reminders of battles fought in imperial wars, I prayed quietly for a kindly outcome to the conflict in the Church being debated in nearby Tanzania and for enlightenment in Zambia as it faced its AIDS epidemic.

Roused by a reflection of the day, I met members of the Law Association of Zambia that evening. I urged them to take on the challenges presented by HIV and AIDS. Where are the Zambian examples in the UNAIDS book of cases, I asked. Judges cannot invent cases. Lawyers must bring them to the courts. They should study what is happening elsewhere. They should challenge unjust laws. Amongst those laws are the ones that criminalise the love of people who are members of sexual minorities.

This group of lawyers, most of them quite young, seemed far more aware of the issues and of the urgency of the battle against HIV and AIDS than the judges had been. Several had been involved in the foundation of ZARAN. Most had been diverted into commercial law. After all, it is here that cases can be fought and won, where the money is good, where the law is without the sensitivities and controversies of the AIDS epidemic. These young lawyers promised they would try to engender a greater sense of urgency. I told them that I would check up on them.

The foundation of all modern movements for the protection of fundamental human rights is the same as that of all of the great religions. It is love. Love for the vulnerable, the poor and those sick of body and heart.

∞

At the airport the following morning, Pablo-of-few-words was enthusiastic about my meeting with the Law Association. He was hopeful that, out of it, would emerge new support for ZARAN, the acceptance of pro bono briefs and the selection of test cases to push the Zambian judiciary in HIV litigation.

He was quieter when I asked him about the seminar. I told him that, in all mighty struggles risks have to be taken. People must be challenged to think freshly. The old thinking had brought his country to its present predicament. My talk to Zambia's judiciary might prove a total failure. Clearly, my ideas were not immediately attractive to their ears. This was fallow territory of the mind: inactive, inert. But one or two of those in the room might consider the issues afresh. Ideas are like that. They burrow away. Sometimes they bring action and change when least expected. And, in any event, the sharing of knowledge was a human obligation.

'Keep steadily in your mind a picture the young man or woman in Zambia infected with HIV. What is their future? How can their tragedy be prevented in others? That will fire you up,' one of my colleagues at UNAIDS in Geneva had told me when I asked what to expect. 'And in any case, you have no choice but to share your knowledge and experience. They must find their own solutions. But for the international community to ignore Zambia is not an option.'

⁓

The plane lifted gracefully into the sunshine. Below me, on the African plateau, lay an anxious country. Of the 1.6 million Zambians who were infected with HIV, thousands of gays and others were ashamed to claim their human rights. I was glad to be on my way home. Out of Africa.

- 7 -

THE SALVOS—
A SURPRISING VISIT TO THE CITADEL

ALTHOUGH I WAS RAISED in the Protestant tradition of Christianity, within the Anglican diocese of Sydney, as I grew up I knew very little about the Salvation Army. I had a dim idea, not wrong as I was to discover, that the Army grew out of Methodism which, in turn, had grown out of the evangelical approach adopted by the brothers John and Charles Wesley in the middle of the eighteenth century. I knew that the Salvos, as everyone called them, were founded by William Booth in the middle of the nineteenth century. Booth became their first general. But beyond that, and knowledge that they did good works for homeless people, alcoholics, the unemployed and the victims of disasters, their faith was a big mystery.

On occasional Sundays in the 1950s, after church, a Salvation Army band would march to the corner of Sydney and Bell Streets in Concord where I was growing up. Their brass instruments gleaming in the late morning sun, they would strike up a lively tune—often, I noticed, a hymn of the Wesley brothers. As, at that time, I had just attended the Methodist Sunday school at the Wesley Church at the top of Sydney Street, I felt that the tunes, and the ethos that the bands espoused, were friendly and familiar; a suitable prelude to the frivolous ice-cream man who seemed to follow the Salvos around with his recorded chimes to gather up the children who were such easy prey to his temptations.

The Salvos were not the mysterious priests and nuns in black from the Roman Catholic Church of St Mary's up there on the hill in Burwood. Yet their military-style uniforms, marching and bands of brass instruments seemed a long way from the stately Anglican church I was to join when I grew old enough to cross the busy Parramatta Road by myself. Somehow, the Salvos' bands appeared a little too modern and undignified. All that oom-pah-pah. Once one became an Anglican, one realised that church music, like everything English, should be quiet, understated and just a little solemn. The Salvos seemed anything but this.

My grandmother Norma, who had worked as a hotel cashier, would occasionally tell us of the Salvos, who were strict teetotallers, coming into her hotel collecting for the down-and-outs and alcoholics. In a robust Australian way, drinkers would welcome them and reach deep into their pockets for some coins. She spoke in praise of them. So did my father who actually went collecting for their Red Shield appeals in Concord and neighbouring places. I did not know whether this was because of theological support for General Booth's practical type of Christianity or because of his gregarious character and desire to make new friends by knocking on new doors. Whatever was his motivation, we were brought up in a tradition that was pretty relaxed and comfortable with the Salvos. There was no affiliation; but certainly no hostility.

∽

Years later, when I was in my late twenties and a very occasional patron of the Rex Hotel, I would see the Salvos enter the Bottoms Up Bar collecting money. Because I knew that these contributions would go to hostels for disadvantaged people and help for alcoholics, I always gave as much as I could. But one day, a gay man nearby demanded angrily to know why I had done that. 'Don't you know that they are homophobes? They attack and discriminate against gays. I wouldn't give them a cent,' he said. This got me thinking.

After that, I would sometimes see representatives of the Salvation Army at ecumenical church services that are quite common in the law. They always seemed to be represented by middle-aged gentlemen, rarely if ever by women. The words of my drinking companion taught me to notice public statements made by the Salvos on issues relating to sexuality. Unfortunately, most of the comments I saw, attributed to leaders of the Salvation Army in Australia, seemed to bear out my friend's warnings. Many of them took a hard line against legal reform of the criminal laws that blighted the lives of gays when I was young. They opposed decriminalisation. And when reform came about, they opposed removal of the discrimination between the age of consent for heterosexuals and homosexuals. They opposed the strategy of harm minimisation for drug users. They rejected the early proposals for needle exchange for injecting drug users that was to prove such an important part of Australia's successful strategy to combat HIV/AIDS.

All in all, when I eventually took notice of the Salvation Army's public statements, I confess to having felt a degree of discomfiture. Their values on some subjects that were close to the heart seemed so different from mine. They did not appear to share the loving, humane principles of the religion of Jesus as I understood it. They seemed rather hard-hearted. Good doers with cold hearts. At least their hearts seemed to be only selectively softened. From time to time I would read of the splendid way in which the Salvos organised themselves to respond quickly to disasters such as Cyclone Tracy that devastated Darwin, and later the Indonesian Tsunami as well as other terrible mishaps. They were usually there first, with friendly well-scrubbed faces, lots of bedding, good organisation. As they sometimes described themselves, they were 'Christianity with its sleeves rolled up'. For the victims of natural disasters, the down-and-outs, unemployed and alcoholics, they were generosity itself. But for gays, drug-dependent persons and women in their Church, they seemed very conservative indeed.

∞

These impressions were reinforced when word spread about the special privileges granted to the Salvos under federal laws and policies introduced by the Howard government in the mid-1990s and afterwards. They became an important vehicle for some of the social services that had previously been undertaken by agencies of the federal government. There was a lot of controversy about the amount of money directed from the Treasury into their pockets and whether they could possibly approach clients in need with complete dispassion when some of them would be the very kind of people they were preaching against and writing about in their published statements on morality.

I did nothing about these controversies. Just filed them away in the back of my mind. They were not my business. But they did serve to dampen my boyhood enthusiasm for the Salvos. I was coming to a view that they were discriminating Christians whilst my own image of the Christian religion involved a notion of undivided love for one another, meaning everybody, not just a chosen few like one's self.

∾

In September 2006, my attitude to the Salvos was put to the test when I received an invitation to participate in a social justice conference being organised by the Australia Eastern Territory of the Army. A young solicitor, Luke Geary, who I was later to find had been baptised and raised as a Roman Catholic, wrote to me to inform me that he had invited Marcus Einfeld to speak at the conference in March 2007. 'Unfortunately,' he said, 'Mr Einfeld has indicated that he is not accepting public appearances at the moment.'

Luke Geary had asked a Queen's Counsel of his acquaintance to recommend a substitute speaker. My name was mentioned and a polite letter enquired whether I would be willing to accept an invitation. The letter indicated that about five hundred people were expected to attend the conference. It would be made up of members of the legal profession, social workers, counsellors, volunteer workers and similar people 'passionate about social justice issues'. The invitation asked me to consider speaking about refugees and advising those attending on how they could act to prevent injustice and otherwise to assist people in need.

Refugee issues presented a tricky problem for me. Such questions were constantly coming before me in the High Court where I was still a sitting judge. I would have to be very careful entering that territory. I thought about the invitation. It would not have been difficult to decline. I was already committed on the evening before to a talk at the Southern Cross University in Lismore. To get back to Sydney in time for the Salvos' conference, I would have to rise with the lark. In the end, however, I thought it could be good both for the Salvos and for myself to have such an encounter. I would get to know some people who were practising members of the Army. It might also be useful for them to get to know a person who was openly gay.

In October 2006 I shot off my reply to Mr Geary. I thanked him for his invitation and said that in the circumstances I would like to help. Nevertheless, I thought it was best to be up-front about the topics that I would tackle if I came along to the conference. So I disclosed a qualification:

> I could not speak on refugee issues or conduct a work-shop, as such issues are constantly coming before the High Court. Nevertheless, I would be willing to talk about social issues from the viewpoint of my participation in a number of United Nations agencies. My topic would be: 'Social Justice—An International Perspective'. In the course of my remarks, I would wish to make reference to social justice to homosexuals and other sexual minorities. I am not sure whether that would fit in with the Salvation Army program. If it would not, it could perhaps be best for you to look for another speaker. If it does, let me know and we will fix an hour for my attendance . . . I pay my respects for the good work that the Salvation Army does for vulnerable and disadvantaged people.

Luke Geary replied to my secretary the next day informing me that the Salvation Army 'would love to have [you] speak at the conference'. He went on indicating 'that the topic suggested would be perfect. I have passed on [your] comments to the other members of the Organising Committee . . . and have had a very enthusiastic response about the topic proposed'. So the die was cast.

∽

The matter went out of my mind as I attended to other commitments. The months passed by. Then, in late January 2007 a letter came to me from the Territorial Commander of the Army in Sydney, Commissioner Les Strong. The letter was polite but quite firm:

> Organisation of this event has been carried out by a team of our people who are developing our social justice portfolio. This awareness-raising conference is their first public platform event and they are doing well with the arrangements.
>
> During this past week I have become aware of a letter from you to our Organisation, in which you outlined some aspects of your planned presentation.
>
> While communication has been issued to you confirming an acceptance of your participation, I have discussed the matter with other senior leaders. It is more appropriate that we activate the escape clause in your letter of October 2006 and withdraw the invitation for you to participate.
>
> Thank you for your willingness to accommodate our conference.

To say that I was surprised to receive this letter would be an understatement. It brought back to me the comment of the fellow drinker at the Rex Hotel thirty years before. The friendly face of the earlier communications seemed suddenly to be replaced with an unwelcoming one. Right or wrong, it seemed a harsh response, out of harmony with the ethos of the religion the Salvos otherwise espoused.

I prepared a letter simply stating that I was greatly saddened and hurt that a Church of Jesus had preferred *not* to hear an address that would include, as one aspect, reference to social justice to those who suffer injustice by reason of their sexuality. But the more I thought about the letter, the more I considered that something a little stronger was required. So I tore up my draft and started again.

In early February 2007 I wrote to Commissioner Strong reminding him that the 'escape clause', to which he had referred, was 'designed to avoid embarrassment to either party before the invitation proceeded'. Having received the reply that the Army would 'love' to have me speak and that the topics I had suggested 'would be perfect', I expressed surprise that four months later the invitation to participate had been withdrawn. I went on:

> I have been in public life since December 1974. I have never previously, in Australia or overseas, had a confirmed invitation to me to speak withdrawn. I am sure that you realise that this is a hurtful gesture. It is one that greatly saddens me, coming as it does from a Church of Jesus.
>
> The Salvation Army, or bodies associated with it, are recipients of substantial federal funds, derived from the taxpayers of Australia in all of their variety. I am sure that it would be a matter of concern to many of our fellow citizens that such a body would withdraw the opportunity of a voice to reflect, amongst other things, at a social justice conference,

the interests of some of the most vulnerable and marginalised in our community.

I am still willing to participate in your conference, as invited and confirmed. I offer my hand in Christian friendship and ask you and your colleagues to reconsider your decision to withdraw the invitation for me to participate. I have no wish to hurt or offend anyone. But surely, in the present age, the Salvation Army that otherwise does such fine work, will not close its ears to the matters described in my letter which initially received such a 'very enthusiastic response'.

∽

I did not really expect the Salvos to change their mind. I know enough about religious people to understand that some currents run very deep. Changing strongly entrenched tradition does not come about simply because of an exchange of letters. Safeguarding five hundred adherents to a Church from what might be a revelation of doctrinal error could prove an overwhelming reason for the commissioner to maintain his position.

The language of 'inerrant scripture' was there as the apparent source of interdiction against any form of same-sex activity. Although there was nothing explicit in the Gospels to this effect attributed to Jesus himself, He had come to fulfil the law, being the law of the Jews. Amongst that law was perhaps the passage in *Leviticus* 20:13, in the Old Testament, forbidding a man who would 'lie with mankind, as he lieth with a woman' and declaring that this was an abomination and that 'they shall surely be put to death, their blood shall be upon them'.

Never mind that so many other provisions of the holiness code in *Leviticus* were now regarded as inapplicable—and certainly no reason for putting a person to death. Never mind that the prohibitions on the blind man, the broken-footed, the crook-backed and the dwarfs now seem alien to the message of the New Testament. Never mind the reference to slaves and wizards and to curses and the countless injunctions to put people to death. The isolated passages, in a literalist interpretation of the Bible, gave apparent support to those in the religions of the Book who still wanted to stigmatise sexual minorities. Having been brought up in the biblical tradition, I knew where the commissioner was coming from. I did not expect a reply.

❧

Soon after I sent my letter, I gave a talk to a young gay audience at a gay venue in Oxford Street, Sydney. I shared their hurt and pain, their complaints of alienation in school, rejection by parents, cold-shoulders from their religion and isolation in society. I tried, as best I could, to encourage them and to sound optimistic. But my encounter with them left me feeling rather depressed and doubtful.

As I walked back to my office from the venue, a dark dance studio by night lit by strobe lights, and out into the sunshine, I came upon a Salvation Army band in Hyde Park. It was playing quietly under trees near the War Memorial, built in the southern part of the park to commemorate the brave sailors, soldiers and airmen who had died in the Great War. I stopped and listened. The band's harmonious music brought back the memories of those Sunday afternoons of my childhood when life seemed so clear and certain.

The mixture of the band's familiar hymns and the recollection of the Army's rejection caught me at a vulnerable moment immediately after my encounter with the hurt and puzzled young gays. For a moment I felt like crying about the obstacles that make it hard to change attitudes to sexual minorities. If good people like the Salvos, otherwise so kind and generous to the vulnerable, turned their backs on gays, how could progress ever be made?

I pulled myself up. Crying would never do. I stiffened my back and walked quickly away. But I felt a sense of loss that in the religion of Jesus—the revolutionary who came with a new covenant—attitudes could be so warped by views about sexuality and by reading in isolation passages of scripture written thousands of years earlier without any of the scientific knowledge we now have concerning sexual orientation in human beings and other mammals.

ॐ

Then, in late February 2007, I received an unexpected letter from Commissioner Strong:

> Further consideration has been given to my earlier communication concerning your participation in the above conference. I have read your letter carefully and regret that my action was considered hurtful. This was certainly not my intention.
>
> Upon reflection and through dialogue with senior colleagues, I do want to rescind the expressed decision contained in my earlier letter and indicate our willingness for you to participate as first requested.
>
> It is my understanding that you will be speaking upon matters of justice from an international perspective. Thank

you for your willingness to give time to this conference which, I believe, will further assist us in meeting the needs of people in our community.

I answered his letter at once. I expressed my pleasure at receiving it. I told the commissioner that when I was in Zambia a few days earlier, I had been told about one of the central figures in the Salvation Army's early response to AIDS, initially from a base in Zambia and later internationally. The commissioner had responded to my request. He had reached out his hand. The arrangements for my attendance at the conference were revived. Luke Geary affirmed how excited a number of people in the Army were about my coming to speak. He told me that Commissioner Strong was looking forward to meeting me there.

At the end of March 2007, on the appointed day, I duly woke with the lark in Lismore. I flew back to Sydney, arriving just on time. Conference participants were milling about. Immediately I was taken upstairs, past some plain rooms in which Army uniforms were laid out, presumably either for new recruits or for those who had come of soldiering age. I joined members of the Army for a cup of tea. I met the session chair, who explained the plan to invite a Salvation Army leader from New Zealand, Major Campbell Roberts, to share the answering of questions directed to me. This was explained as being intended to ensure that any 'arcane' points of Salvation Army doctrine could be explained. Was this acceptable? Far from resenting this, I welcomed such cooperation.

∽

I walked into the large room in the Sydney Congress Hall. From the stage it looked like a big city cinema, but without the luxury. It was a place of hard benches and simple faith. This was the plain, unadorned environment that the Sydney Anglicans also try to observe, but without the serious obstacles to that endeavour often caused by stonework and stained-glass windows. There were popular songs, accompanied by young men on guitars. None of the grand organs of the churches of my youth. But I did not feel alien in that place. Indeed, as I told the audience when I spoke, I knew where their faith was coming from. I had been brought up in similar simplicities. I had been taught to reject pretension and to beware of alcohol and gambling.

My speech unfolded in a spontaneous way. Afterwards, Major Campbell Roberts joined me on the stage for questions. Many of the questions were tangential to my themes. But at one point, after a warming up in the audience, a young female soldier rose. She asked whether there were gay soldiers in the Salvation Army. What was the Army doing to help and support them? Should they not be encouraged and supported to have their own loving relationships? Indeed, should there not be marriages for them, as for other soldiers? These were the questions of a young person of a new generation. You could almost hear a gasp in the hall. Perhaps these were the very questions the Army had originally preferred not to be asked.

∾

Before the conference I had secured a copy of the statement of the Salvation Army on human sexuality. It is posted on the Army's website. Beginning in a kindly enough fashion, it contained few surprises.

The Salvation Army seeks to understand, accept and lovingly minister to all people, recognising the depth and intensity of feeling about sexual identity, as well as the attendant pain and difficulties sometimes experienced in living in harmony with God's standards.

It is the Salvation Army's belief that whilst recognising the possibility of [homosexual] orientation (the origins of which are uncertain), the Bible expressly opposes homosexual practice, seeing such activity as rebellion against God's plan for the created order . . .

A disposition towards homosexual is not in itself blameworthy nor is the disposition seen as rectifiable at will. The Army is sensitive to the complex social, emotional and spiritual needs of all people including those with homosexual inclinations. We oppose vilification of, or discrimination against, anyone on the grounds of sexual orientation. No person is excluded from membership, fellowship or service in the Army solely on the basis of sexual disposition.

However, it then goes on:

Homosexual practice, however, is, in the light of Scripture, clearly unacceptable. Such activity is chosen behaviour and thus a matter of the will . . . Homosexual practice would render any person ineligible for full membership (soldier-ship) in the Army. However, practising homosexuals are welcome to worship with, and join in the fellowship of, the Salvation Army.

The statement refers to the well-known passage in *Leviticus*, to passages in *Genesis* and to others in the writings of Paul. The hard part is the statement that homosexual practice is 'clearly unacceptable'. May this not, I thought, require some reconsideration and elaboration in the light of the acknowledgment that homosexuality is an orientation, that it is not capable of change at will, and that it causes deep and intense feelings, as much in homosexuals as in heterosexuals?

∾

In answer to the female questioner, I suggested that it would be necessary to secure change in the Army's position on these issues, step by step but in harmony with the scientific knowledge that we now have. Major Roberts added that in New Zealand, the Salvation Army, twenty years earlier, had been one of the strongest opponents of repeal of the criminal laws against homosexual acts. It had campaigned strongly against the change. Recently, without denying the traditional understandings of scripture, the New Zealand Army had apologised for some of the things done and said at that time. Major Roberts suggested that, by dialogue and more contact, greater knowledge would come about. I indicated that this was one of the reasons why I had come to participate in the dialogue with the Australian Salvation Army.

At the close of my remarks I reminded the audience that during the preceding week Anthony Callea, a popular runner-up for *Australian Idol*, had acknowledged he was gay. As a young Italian–Australian man, this would not have been easy for him—no easier than for a young Salvation Army soldier. I reminded the audience, most of whom were young, that he had a big hit with his song 'The Prayer'. Reportedly, it was one of the highest selling songs in Australian popular music chart history. The words were apt for the occasion—so I read them to the quietened audience. It finished with the prayer, 'When we lose our way, we hope you will guide us with your grace'.

The dialogue with the Salvos was concluded. The applause was generous. Everyone seemed relieved that we had got through the session without disasters. The Salvos were respectful to me. I was respectful to them. In particular, I recognised that things long established sometimes take time to change, but change they should. Commissioner Strong came up after the talk. He shook my hand and thanked me for my 'sensitivity'. I took this to mean sensitivity to the Salvos' positions. But Major Campbell Roberts's words rang through the meeting hall. If the Salvationists were now apologising in New Zealand for errors in what they said and did twenty years ago, might not change come for Salvationists in Australia? Perhaps when the simple scientific truths are placed alongside the words of scripture understanding will follow.

∾

I walked back into the sunshine of an autumn morning across the park humming 'The Prayer'. There was no band playing in the leafy corner near the War Memorial. No brass instruments gleamed in the sunlight. But perhaps a few hearts and minds were opened that day. And maybe someone in that hall, or in the meetings to be reached by the recording of what we said that day, will feel less lonely and isolated.

Love helps to solve all problems. Human beings, reflecting on their own needs for love, can usually find in themselves an understanding of the needs for love of others. Perhaps especially good people—doers—like the Salvos.

THE PRINCE—IN DANGEROUS TIMES

RAJPIPLA IS A TOWN in the Narmada District of Gujarat in western India. Unlike many towns in that part of India, it is blessed with abundant and reliable rainfall and watered by a river that flows nearby. Central to the life of Rajpipla is the Vijay Palace. It is the home of the local royal family who are still revered in those parts.

Until independence from the British came to India in 1947, the country was a patchwork quilt of princely states with only a few large areas ruled directly by the British Crown. For the most part, the pale and aloof rulers of the Raj were content to hold sway over their Indian Empire, and to exert their dominion, through the princes. Those princes were themselves often the descendants of the great Mogul Empire of Delhi, the disintegration of which was both the cause of, and the opportunity for, expanded British rule. As Rosita Forbes wrote in 1939 in her book *India of the Princes*, 'Out of the chaos rose, by an unparalleled feat of history, the states and the ruling Princes of today'.

About a quarter of the population of the Empire of India, at the time of independence from the British, were subjects of the princely states. Nearly two-fifths of the geographical area of the subcontinent was within the domain of more than five hundred princely houses. Until 1947 the most important of them were linked to the British Crown by treaty. Counting every small fiefdom ruled by semi-independent chieftains, there were actually some six hundred and fifty such states. Amongst these, only seventy-three of the princes were entitled to salutes of more than eleven guns and to the prefix of 'highness'.

In British days the largest of the princely states were Hyderabad and Kashmir. By one of the ironies of history, each of these states had a prince whose religion was the reverse of that of the majority of his subjects. Hyderabad's nizam, the title given to that state's sovereign, was a Muslim, but 90 per cent of the people living there were Hindus. In Kashmir, the maharaja was of Rajput origin, a Hindu. But nearly 90 per cent of his subjects were Muslim. In those two states were laid down some of the conflicts that still exist on the face of the Indian subcontinent today.

In a last gesture of respect for the princes of India, the British left it to them to opt for the successor dominion of their choice—whether India or Pakistan. The nizam opted for Pakistan. However, his landlocked state was soon occupied by Indian military forces. Hyderabad then acceded, as commonsense and geography demanded, to India. In Kashmir, the maharaja opted for India. The warring armies marked out a battleline in the mountainous reaches of Kashmir which is still largely in place. The division need not have happened if only the Indian negotiators had been a little more patient and had more time and willingness to compromise on their side.

Under the independence constitution of India, confirmed in the republican instrument of freedom, the princes of India were initially guaranteed privy purses in return for surrendering their sovereignty to the new nation. These purses were declared to be theirs in perpetuity. In this respect, Rajpipla was no different from the others. The maharaja, who opted for India, released his subjects so that they could hold their allegiance to the new nation. In return, the princes were promised tax-free revenue and, according to their rank, a certain influence in the new nation. Yet with the passage of the years after independence, these promises were undone. Increasingly, the princes looked anachronistic and out of touch with the radical sensibilities of India of the Congress Party led by Jawaharlal Nehru.

The twenty-sixth amendment to the Constitution of India was adopted in 1971. It abolished the privy purses guaranteed by the former Dominion of India. The repeal of the constitutional covenants and agreements with the rulers of the Indian states was challenged as a betrayal of trust in the Supreme Court. The challenge was rejected. Now, the princes in republican India were denied not only the allegiance of their subjects and official status but also income. If they were to have a place in the modern world they had to earn that place, in part from their investments and in part by winning and keeping the respect of the people who had previously owed them allegiance.

❧

The Gohil Rajput dynasty that ruled Rajpipla found itself in a better position than many of the princes. Its state, in the foothills of the Satpur Range, comprised forests and fertile agricultural plains, spanning an area of over 2500 square kilometres. It was second only to Baroda, in south-eastern Gujarat, as one of the most prosperous princely states in the western part of India. As well, the Gohils earned respect as modernisers. They had adapted skilfully to the British hegemony. After the suppression of the uprising of 1857, which the British called 'the mutiny', they embraced progressive values, at least during the last decades of the nineteenth century.

By the time of the Great Durbar of 1911, which saw the King Emperor George V and his Queen Empress Mary honoured by the Indian princes in Delhi, the ruler of Rajpipla was very highly regarded. In 1915, his successor, Vijay Singh ascended to the throne. In due course the prince was appointed Knight Commander of the Order of the Indian Empire with the title of 'maharaja'. The gun salutes for the ruler of Rajpipla were increased at that time from eleven to thirteen. This placed the maharaja amongst the foremost princes of the Indian Empire.

The Gohil family also boasted a 600-year royal heritage. This meant producing descendants with modern relevance. The reigning Maharaja of Rajpipla was the biggest land owner of the district in 2007. He owned then several palaces, full of ancient heirlooms, priceless china and sumptuous royal costumes. Maharaja Roghubir Singhji followed family tradition by selecting his bride, a princess from a neighbouring state. She became the maharani. A son was born to the marriage, Manvendra. By convention he is usually still called 'prince'.

As the only son and heir presumptive to the traditions of the Gohil dynasty, the young prince enjoyed a most privileged upbringing. It was naturally assumed that, in due course, he would take over the duties of the royal house. He would administer its wealth. But he would also act as a supporter of education, a community leader and patron of the local arts. At the age of twenty-two, the young Prince Manvendra married a princess chosen for him by his mother. The bride, as a princess, hailed from the state of Madhya Pradesh. To outsiders, everything looked like a fairytale. Inside the palaces, however, things were rather different.

As he grew up, the young Manvendra discovered that his sexual attraction was to his own sex. Reportedly, he experimented with a servant boy of his own age. It was their secret. However, after his marriage, it became much more difficult to sustain the lie. Eventually, unwilling to keep up the pretence any longer, Manvendra's princess asked him for a divorce. This was agreed to. 'Don't ever do that again to another girl,' she told him, as they parted.

Manvendra made a few cautious moves to explore the gay nightlife in Mumbai where his family had a city residence. In 2002, the prince engaged a psychiatrist who arranged a family meeting to explain Manvendra's sexual orientation. Even this passed without causing too many waves along the Narmada River. But then things changed.

Manvendra, a highly intelligent man, had inherited, you will understand, a princely sense of obligation. He saw the absurdity of the provisions in the Indian penal code, originally imposed by the British, which punished adult private consensual sexual conduct as serious crimes. As well, he came to interest himself in the special challenges confronting his domains after the arrival of HIV, the agent that causes the often fatal condition AIDS. As more of Manvendra's fellow citizens became infected, he knew that he had to do something. What Manvendra decided to do was something very unusual for a prince living in a palace where even a glass of water was procured for him on bended knee.

Seizing an opportunity in 2006, the prince spoke to a local newspaper in Rajpipla revealing he was gay. The news was splashed across the front page. Very soon it was taken up by the *Times of India* and many of the national dailies. India is a land of newspapers. Most people who can do so read at least one broadsheet a day. Before long Manvendra's revelation was circling around the world. A prince in India was gay. No news in that. But this prince was candid and outspoken about it. Moreover, he was chairing an organisation, the Lakshya Trust, dedicated to educating Indians about HIV and the prevention of the spread of AIDS. In the land of *Kamasutra*, where no one speaks openly of sex and where HIV had already spread amidst a deafening silence to five million men, women and children, this was truly news. Big news.

The story of Manvendra's coming out was eventually carried in the *International Herald Tribune*. It was there that I read for the first time that the prince's mother had refused to speak to him for disgracing not only the Rajpipla dynasty but all of the royal houses of India. In faraway Australia, I felt an empathy for this man, and a certain admiration. Could Prince Manvendra perhaps be persuaded to give leadership in India, and beyond, for the battle against HIV? After all, most people like a prince.

∽

Early in 2007 it was arranged that I would travel to India to participate in seminars about HIV and the law. I suggested to the organisers, the Mumbai-based Lawyers Collective working to raise consciousness about HIV and AIDS, that we should engage with the prince. As it happened, Manvendra had attended an earlier meeting in Mumbai organised by this sponsor. There, he had seen me and Justice Edwin Cameron from South Africa. He had not introduced himself at the time. He was still then in the twilight zone between acknowledgment to his family and announcement to the world. Now he was enthusiastic for a meeting. So the arrangements were explored.

On the day before I was due to leave India, Prince Manvendra was at his palace in Rajpipla. It is difficult for those unfamiliar with India to realise the central place that railways still play in the movement of millions of people in the subcontinent each and every day. The prince offered to come by train to Mumbai to meet me. However, I was planning a visit to Bassein, north of the city, on the morning of my last day. Host to a large Portuguese fort that earlier guarded the first European empire in those parts, Bassein is now a thriving town caught up in the great economic progress seen everywhere around Mumbai. Once, not so long ago, it was a sleepy fishing village.

When Bombay (as Mumbai was called until 1997) was ceded to Britain by Portugal as part of the dowry of Charles II's Portuguese bride, Catherine of Braganza, it carried with it, somewhat reluctantly on their part, the Portuguese fort at Bassein. The walls and churches, the administrative buildings and guarded citadels were all handed over. However, they were of no further use to the new rulers who allowed them to fall into decay. British power in western India lay elsewhere, to the south in the glittering metropolis they built in Bombay.

In 1970, on my first visit to Bombay with Johan, we travelled to Bassein. Then it was nothing more than a sandy village. The ghostly fortifications stood bleak and forbidding as a reminder of times past. There was something eerie about the carvings of the royal coat of arms of Portugal and the abandoned churches that once had been filled with Latin-chanting priests and a religion that had somehow failed to conquer this corner of the world. Bassein looked rather like a smaller, run-down version of Goa, further down the same coast to the south. It was off the beaten track. Few tourists visited it. On later journeys to Mumbai, I would often take the train from Churchgate Station to Vasai, as Bassein is now called by the locals. In 2007, I wanted to walk once again over the walls of the old fort. So I proposed to meet Prince Manvendra in Bassein. I doubt if he would ever have heard of it. In the turbulent world of his India, the abandoned relics of long forgotten Portuguese rule would not have figured highly in the calendar of princely priorities.

∽

On its journey south to Mumbai, the prince's train from Rajpipla did not condescend to stop at Vasai, for it was such a minor station. However, it did stop across the river in a larger town. So the prince told me that a local train would bring him to Bassein where we agreed to meet up. At the crack of dawn, we each arose and repaired to a bustling railway station to catch our respective trains for our rendezvous. I told the prince that I would wait near the booking office on the fort side of Vasai's station. He estimated his own arrival at 10 a.m.

I duly arrived near a sign at the Vasai station that bore the legend of the great train services that crossed India every day. There timetables conjured up images of times past. The Deccan Express still passes through Bassein every morning. You can take a train at midnight that eventually draws into the great railway stations in Madras, now called Chennai, and in Calcutta, now Kolkatta. At all hours of the day and night the trains come and go. A mass of humanity swirls and then disappears into the carriages. New passengers appear out of nowhere to purchase tickets for trains to places near and far.

Some of the passengers who swept past me that morning were dressed in saffron robes. Many were business people in suits. A few workers carried their tiffin boxes. Many students passed me by listening to their iPods, fully in touch with the twenty-first century. I was in the midst of an extraordinary kaleidoscope of humanity: a microcosm of amazing India.

I had time to fill in. So I walked to the platform where shoeshiners banged their little boxes to attract attention. All offered cut prices to do the honours on my leather. The one I chose even threw in replacement shoe laces after he had removed every speck of dust and grime. I tipped him handsomely and was rewarded with a brilliant smile. I then walked for a while around the town that had grown up next to the railway platforms. The change from my first visit in 1970 was astonishing. Modern shops had been built, yet most of the roads were still unpaved or had been broken up by heavy trucks. Scenes of ordered chaos were everywhere. I looked for a place worthy of a prince to breakfast. None on offer sprang to attention. So I postponed the search and hurried back to the booking hall to wait the royal arrival, for the hour of his train was approaching.

As I examined the faces of the crowd I tried to imagine what the prince would look like. The only photo I had seen of him, on the internet, showed him with a fine ceremonial golden turban. I hardly expected him to turn up in Bassein wearing that. Although he continued to live in the palace, I imagined the supply of flunkies might have been dropped away since his outing. Searching the faces of modern India for the face of a prince, basically of unknown appearance, proved somewhat challenging.

Every now and then, I would see a man standing alone. Perhaps this was the prince, I thought. But then a companion would arrive and off they would go laughing and talking.

In railway stations, Indians are generally well behaved. Sheer numbers demand it. They queue patiently. They wait their turn. I watched people line up for tickets moving closer to the counter and then disappear onto the platforms and the waiting trains. Curiously, the windows were placed very low, perhaps built at a time when Indians generally were shorter. Today's generation had to bow as they barked their demands for tickets.

⁓

Half an hour late, a thin man looking younger than his forty years, dressed in simple traditional clothes, arrived. 'Manvendra,' he said, and thrust out his hand.

Prince Manvendra Singh Gohil stood on that fragile borderline between youth and middle years. His face looked distinguished. His hair was still black and he sported a dark moustache. His eyes were his most striking feature. Brown and somewhat sad. He had long fingers and carried a little bag with water and the needs for his onward journey down to the family residence near Mumbai's airport at Santa Cruz.

I enquired whether he had taken his breakfast on the train. He had not, so we went in search of a suitable restaurant on the far side of the station. Bassein, as I had discovered, was not like central Mumbai with its pristine eating places sheltering behind glass and boasting aircon. The best we could find was an open-air restaurant beside a dusty road where noisy trucks passed by constantly, and occasional beggars presented their hands demanding alms.

Manvendra ordered a traditional Indian breakfast. I ordered eggs. The waiter went away but soon returned to tell me that eggs were not available as the kitchen was still closed. There were flies everywhere and I became grateful that eggs were off the menu. I settled for a cup of tea but without the sickly milk and sugar concoction of these parts. We talked of Manvendra's life, of his family and of the organisation he now heads. I noticed that it was only when we discussed the Lakshya Trust that his eyes brightened up.

Life in the palace, it appeared, was still fraught. In the early days after his outing, Manvendra's parents had announced that the prince was disinherited, an assertion seemingly of questionable legal effect. His mother had cut him off and still refused to speak to him. Relations with his father were better. The Maharaja had sold the traditional princely bungalow in Santa Cruz and built a modern complex with an apartment for the royal family when they were in town. At one stage he acted as a consul in Mumbai for a Caribbean state, taking him to Mumbai for much of his time. This gave him the opportunity to become close to his son, away from palace tensions.

It was Manvendra's modesty that most struck me. He told me of his admiration and gratitude after he had attended the earlier meeting in Mumbai. 'You have your title by your effort and distinction,' he said. 'Mine is just an accident of history. It is an anachronism. Yet I want to do something for myself that is worthy. A silver spoon by birth is not enough. I want to contribute to the lives of others. And that is why I decided to establish an organisation to help in the struggle against AIDS. It has won awards for its work for MSMs [men who have sex with men] in Gujarat state.'

I was impressed that Manvendra was so up to date with the official language of United Nations reports. In the structured and unprivate society of India, where having sex is often difficult, the labels 'gay' or 'queer' or 'homosexual' are for many MSMs, representative of western decadence. The use of MSM means these terms can be avoided.

The prince told me he and his mother now rarely meet. Their communications were generally through intermediaries. His mother had obviously known her only son was gay, many members of Indian royal houses were. However, acknowledging his sexuality to the world was not the kind of thing a member of a royal house in India ever did. She felt shame and fear. He should have just gone on pretending, acting the part. That, after all, is something that royals are expected to do all the time.

Worst of all, from his mother's point of view, was Manvendra's active involvement in the Lakshya Trust, a body concerned with the riffraff, including MSM. Unspeakable. The maharani demanded Manvendra give up his association with the trust. That was to ask him to cross a bridge too far.

As I watched the prince speak of his mother, I witnessed an even greater sadness. Clearly he loved and respected her. She was, by his account, an educated and intelligent woman. 'This is a family matter,' he declared. 'Like most families we will sort things out eventually. I never speak ill of my mother.' I sensed Manvendra had experienced a difficult upbringing. Around the palace at Rajpipla he is always addressed by his title. He, in turn, always refers to his father and mother by their titles, never 'Mum' or 'Dad'. When I remarked that this seemed somewhat impersonal he replied that it was just the world in which he was brought up. For him it was perfectly normal. Just like the servants and the deference, it was all that he had ever known.

We talked for an hour and Manvendra proudly showed me a photograph of the award ceremony where he and colleagues in the Lakshya Trust had been honoured for their work in the struggle against HIV. Clearly, this was now the centre of his life. At last, it seemed, he had found a purpose—one devised by him, not handed to him in a silver platter. As I studied the photograph, I wondered how the maharajas at the Great Durbar of 1911 would have reacted at learning that one of their descendants was down on the streets, trying to educate MSMs and others at the front-line of the battle against a brutal new epidemic. Some, I suspected, would had understood Manvendra's motivation and applaud his modernity. Others, probably most, would react as his mother had. For them, leadership was polo and property, garden parties and the arts. It would have had absolutely nothing to do with sex. Yet with five million Indians infected, contemporary leadership surely needs a person with Manvendra's gifts walking down the difficult road of HIV education.

∽

I told Manvendra about the Bassein Fort built by the Portuguese on the coast about three kilometres away. As I expected, he had never seen it. I asked him if he wanted to accompany me on my visit. I half expected that it would be of no interest to a descendant of the Rajputs to view the relic of foreign rule on the coast of his land. However, Manvendra wanted to continue our conversation, so was willing to tolerate my curious fascination with the remnants of a faded empire. Not even his own.

We left the restaurant and the flies. He insisted on paying for the humble breakfast. We crossed the railway line and walked through shops by then full of customers. Smiling, he agreed to be photographed in front of a life-size poster of a handsome Indian man in briefs decorating the window of a menswear shop. 'I had noticed that too,' he said, laughing. We found an auto-rickshaw. When the driver turned around, I could see the features of the long-departed Portuguese written on his face. He was, perhaps, a descendant of the sailors and soldiers who had built the Bassein Fort. Now he was taking a prince and an Australian foreigner on the bumpy journey towards the handiwork of some of his forebears.

Our driver could not wait for us for the return trip as he had to go to the hospital where his wife was expecting their child. For a few moments I had visions of our being abandoned at the fort and a long walk back to the town. Auto-rickshaws were plentiful everywhere in India the prince reassured me. I was not to be afraid.

The road hugged the river. In the distance, at the end of a promontory, loomed the fort. The external walls of black stone were still in fairly good repair. Battered by four centuries of monsoons and now covered by trees whose roots had worked their way through its crevices, the fort still looked strong to an inexpert eye. As we came closer to it, however, the decay became more apparent.

I remembered how, on earlier journeys, the final approach had been along a sandy track. Now, the track was macadamised. On each side there were shops and schools and the colourful paraphernalia of modern Indian life. The rustic community of the fishermen in 1970 had given way to the developments of contemporary India. No longer was this a backwater. Now, it was virtually an outer suburb of Mumbai.

I gained the impression that for the people living around the fort its presence was something of a nuisance. Doubtless it was protected as a historical monument by the Survey of India under a law of the government of India, so homes and shops and schools could not be built within its walls. For a moment I felt sad that contemporary reality was now battering up against the Portuguese fantasy. No longer did the fort stand preserved by its uniqueness. Modern life, like a kind of cancer, was coming forward to claim back even Bassein Fort. I tried to conjure in my mind the images of the artisans—Portuguese and Indians—who had first built the walls. The priests and the monks who worshipped in the churches. The scurrying merchants struggling to establish a viable economy. The soldiers in their gaudy uniforms, demanding respect from all who crossed their paths. Now gone.

∽

Manvendra, who was used to historical places of his own, seemed not wholly interested in the fort as we walked the last distance towards the ruins. At the church, we climbed the turrets and looked over the fort walls. We could see the broad river that still flowed down to the Arabian Sea, just as it had done in Portuguese and then in British days, and later independence.

We sat there for half an hour talking. He wanted to know how he could do more to help protect India and its people from HIV and AIDS. He spoke of love and life and of his search for both. I told him of my own fortunate search and discovery of companionship and love. He was interested in this story. However, he kept his reserve, as princes do I suppose. I did not press him for stories of his own life. Surrounded by the graves of proud Portuguese conquerors, it somehow seemed inappropriate, an impermissible indulgence. Clearly, Manvendra had turned his back on falsehood. Yet he knew the dangers and difficulties of too much openness in India. The empire fused together, in a terrible alchemy, the hypocrisy of two nations expert in deception. Manvendra was aware of the obstacles he had to overcome. And he was clearly determined to try.

We descended the circular stone staircase from the church tower. He was taller than I but we both had to lower our heads to get through the arch built for the nuggetty Portuguese warriors of earlier times. We passed a water well where young men were washing themselves, their brown bodies gleaming in the sunlight. One of the men agreed to take a photograph of the prince and me under a decrepit arch—all that was left of the guarded entrance to the safety of the fort. We thanked him and went on our way to a circle of auto-rickshaws. There had been no need for my fear of abandonment. Our new driver returned us to the railway station. The Bassein Fort receded in sight and memory.

On the journey we took together back to Mumbai, Manvendra told me that he would send a present to Johan. It would be a piece of handiwork of the indigenous tribes who lived not far from the Rajpipla palace. He was keen to support their work.

We descended from the suburban train on the outskirts of Mumbai. Heartily, Mavendra shook my hand. I paid my respects to him. Those respects were not given to him because he was a prince. They were given because he was a human being who had decided to be true to himself and to strive to do brave things for others.

⌒

To be the first anything is often difficult. To be the first prince of India to come out as gay took a lot courage. To turn the rejection of his mother and the contempt of others into positive action in an urgent cause is an inspiring example of human determination in the face of many odds. To appear on Oprah's television program in America, and speak of his life and work in India contributed to a global struggle, greater than he probably knew. History will judge Prince Manvendra well. I would not be surprised if, in future years, he comes to play an honoured part in the life of his country and of a wider world. AIDS can only be contained by ruthless honesty. Hiding reality is, or should be, over. In India, where most of the politicians and leaders are still silent, it took a prince to see the truth and to tell it as it is.

- 9 -

BUGGER THE ROSES—
REFLECTIONS ON RELATIVITIES

THE OTHER DAY WE had an old friend to dinner. He is a judge, and in his sixties I suppose. He is a bit of a closet case, I'm afraid. But not alone in that regard. When Johan and I decided to put our relationship in *Who's Who in Australia*, we asked him what he thought. 'Don't do it!' he exclaimed. 'If you put your head above the parapet, the nasties and the loonies will take a shot at you.' We went ahead anyway and are glad that we did.

After Senator Bill Heffernan's attack on me in the Senate, the judge got in touch with us and said, with just a little too much self-satisfaction, 'There, I told you so. Red rag to the bull. Everyone knows there are gays out there. But you inflame them if you decline to be thoroughly ashamed of yourself.' I could understand his comment. But it made Johan livid. Our dinner party with him was a kind of reconciliation.

When the time came for farewells, the judge rose and embraced us both with a hug and a kiss. 'Never thought I'd be kissing two seventy-two year old men,' he lamented as he walked to the door. 'And lusting after one of them' was Johan's reply, referring by inference to himself. His Honour did not know whether to laugh or blush.

I doubt that an equivalent statement would be made at most straight dinner parties. Perhaps this is the peculiar feature of gay discourse. Irony, sarcasm. Often with a sexual edge, even if it is self-mocking. Growing old is not something one plans. It just happens, if you are lucky enough to hang on. For most of my life, I was the youngest this and the youngest that. But now there is no getting away from it. I am ancient. Still, I don't plan to go down without a fight.

For some reason, I can remember distinctly a particular moment when I was studying Arts at Sydney University. A trick of memory, I suppose. I was near the Great Hall, a large sandstone pile that is set off by a lovely lawn near the Botany School where Professor John Anderson taught Murray Gleeson and me Philosophy in 1956. Long before our judicial glories. I was only seventeen and had never been kissed. Not that way, at least.

Looking across at the lawn, I noticed a handsome man stretched out in the sunshine. 'How old is he?' I asked a companion. 'I'd say about thirty.' 'God! Thirty! He's as old as Methuselah,' I declared. That is the sort of attitude young people have towards age. Age is at least fifteen years older than oneself. Perhaps this is the procreative space that separates one generation from the next. Today, a man of thirty lying in the sunshine is tantalisingly young. Proving once again that reality is a matter of relativities, just as Einstein taught.

As it happens, I embarked on my long journey with Johan when we were both on the cusp of thirty. I had just been abandoned by my first partner, the gorgeous Spaniard Demo. He had stuck it out for seven months, although he never actually lived with me fulltime. We went to New Zealand together. And when we came back, he left. Suddenly. And there I was, on the shelf, Methuselah-like, and nearly thirty. Just like the old man on the Botany lawn. It was in such a state of desperation that I met Johan and we have been together ever since.

At the time of our meeting, neither of us had older gay friends. Don't forget that the 1970s was a time of criminal sanctions against gay people, public humiliation and denigration. There may have been circles of oldies, but we didn't know them. Before that fateful night of our meeting, Johan had only been twice to the Rex Hotel in Kings Cross. In all, I had only been maybe ten or fifteen times to the handful of gay venues I had discovered in Sydney. My life as a young barrister was just too busy and pre-occupied. Then, as now, I had to be tucked into bed by 10 o'clock. But nothing happens in the gay venues, nothing at all, before midnight.

This timetable partially sorts out the young from the old. Putting it as gently as I can, one must admit that older roses tend to fold up after dusk. Doing the rounds of the gay venues before I met Demo and Johan, I would occasionally spy ancient warriors who sometimes seemed to have a coterie of young admirers around them. Once, I even saw a judge in the Rex Hotel, quietly sipping a beer. I was not sure whether to be horrified that he was in a pub (then against the rules for judges) or in a gay bar. Anyway, our eyes did not meet. And if he saw me, he politely pretended to ignore the fact.

Partly because of inclination and partly for reasons of prudence and discretion, once my relationship with Johan was established, we basically became a boring suburban couple. I am not saying that life was without adventures. But on the whole, we quickly found that we preferred our own company and the company of a very small circle of close friends. Most of them are about our age. They have grown old with us and there would be no more than ten or so. None is older than us. When, occasionally, I have suggested inviting this or that person for dinner, Johan will usually protest: 'But they are young enough to be our children, if not our grandchildren. It would be horrible, most horrible, for them.' So the invitations rarely issue.

As soon as we met, I discovered that Johan loved history. Every night, he was propped up in bed reading a new book, often on history or a biography. Many about Europe. Some about Asia and the Middle East, where we were soon to travel. With excitement, he would then begin to tell me stories from the books. He became, and still is, a kind of living reader's digest, taking pity on the fact that my busy life prevented me from reading as much as he did. He can admire a beautiful young person as much as I, but he always cautions me: 'After the messy business is over, I somehow doubt that he could engage in a discussion about the early Etruscans.'

In our early days together, we would occasionally visit the handful of gay cabarets on offer at that time. The highlight of our week in the early 1970s would be a visit to the *Purple Onion*. There, in suburban Kensington, David Williams would perform in drag as Carmen, hilariously fluttering those long eyelashes as he went through his paces. But this was really a transient leftover from the routine Demo had established with me. Soon, when new performers replaced our familiar favourites, Johan and I retreated into our citadel. It was a place of calm and reassurance in a busy and often stressful life.

At home, in the 1970s, we would sit watching the television with our dinner on trays, glued to the weekly episodes of *No. 96* on Channel 10. An otherwise mediocre soap opera about the residents in a Sydney inner suburb resonated with us. It was the first time we had ever seen gay characters portrayed on the screen leading normal lives and not killed off by suicide after a few episodes. Until then that had been the fate usually reserved for homosexuals. The handsome, young, straight Australian actor Joe Hasham, who played the gay neighbour, did more good for the cause of acceptance than all the learned speeches of advocates for gay reform. Ironically, he was later to make his mark on television in Malaysia where, to this day, it is forbidden by law to portray gays sympathetically. Now, even the handsome Joe is, presumably, old. But we owe him a debt.

Suddenly, three years ago, we stopped watching television, I virtually completely. Johan still takes in *Fox and Friends* because he says he needs it to raise his blood pressure. But now we have rediscovered the joy of conversation over dinner, just as we did in the two years when we were travelling overland in our Kombi vans. He still tells me of the books he is reading. And I describe the events of my day. Now I look back with some regrets at the time we wasted watching banal programs on television. So much more interesting, and stimulating, to explore the mind and feelings of one's life companion. We have shared a big adventure together. Most of it has been enjoyable. During the years when we were obliged to deny our reality in public, in a funny way, this threw us into a special closeness, simply because we knew that society expected us to deny our truth. We would not wish that on young gay people today. But it did have that unintended side-effect. The closeness was reinforced in the 1980s by the loss of many of our gay friends to AIDS. In the 1990s, it was strengthened during the sometimes difficult years of life in Canberra.

If I had not been homosexual, I would almost certainly have married and had children and grandchildren. In the immortal words of the hero in *Zorba the Greek*, I would have enjoyed the 'full catastrophe'. I am just that sort of uxorious person. As I have lately been reminded by a biographer, in fundamentals I am a little conservative. But having such a long-term relationship with Johan has been a great blessing. Such a life is good for human beings physically and psychologically. Those who deny legal and social reinforcement for such relationships are basically formalists who do not care a toss for the scientific evidence about sexual variation and disdain a cohort of their fellow citizens simply because they are different.

Had I not been gay, I do not believe that my social and personal values would have been all that different. Almost certainly, I would support gay people and their causes, just as my brothers and sisters, and now my father, have done. I was brought up with liberal social values. This was the ethos of our home as children. Basically, I was taught to love my neighbour. But I will not go there because religion is a constant source of constructive disagreement between my partner and me. He's against it.

Apart from the emotional, physical and intellectual relationship I have enjoyed with Johan, I have been fortunate in many true friends and countless acquaintances. My life in the courts was sometimes stressful but usually intensely interesting. Every day, for more than three decades, my job involved me in trying to solve puzzles. What were the facts of the matter? What was the relevant law? How should the law be applied to the facts? What was the lawful and just outcome? Not everybody wants a job of solving problems. Many people would regard such a life as the pits. Especially because, at least with judges, they cannot delegate their functions, as they grow older, to be performed by others.

It used to be said that that was why, in Washington, the quality of the output of the judiciary was so much better than the other branches of government, because they wrote their own opinions. In Washington, but not yet Australia, this has changed. So the judge's mind is constantly engaged with perplexing stories and trying to make sense and justice of them all.

For some judges, these puzzles were not sufficient stimulus. I well remember that Mary Gaudron, Justice of the High Court of Australia for sixteen years, had chambers next to mine. She would begin every day with the challenge of the cryptic crossword. Exercising the brain tends to ward off mental decline. A research project once showed that French nuns who spent their lives in penitent meditation and saying the rosary suffered much more mental decline much more quickly than those who added to the ingredients an occasional game of bridge. How unkind of God to do that to them. But Mary was taking no chances. Every day it was the cryptic crossword first and then the appeal second.

Having healthy genes is another blessing. At ninety-five, my father recently gained a renewal of his driver's licence. The testing instructor told him that his driving had actually improved in the two years between tests. So, unsurprisingly perhaps, having 'retired' from my judicial post has not led me to a life of inactivity. On the contrary, as the saying goes, I have never been busier: with international committees, mediations and arbitrations, conferences, professorships, books and other chores.

Until now, Johan has to some extent been house-bound by the series of Abyssinian cats that have lived with us these past thirty-five years. Now, only one is left, Sheba. She is nineteen years old. Johan claims that she sits on the bed staring at him as if demanding to know who will go first. Cats, of course, are only one-person animals. Sheba barely tolerates me. But she loves

Johan and the feeling is mutual. Recently, he took her to the vet and was assured that she would probably outlast us both. This being the case, it seems that we are stuck with Sheba. If she dies and joins the cats' heaven in the sky, Johan will be able to join me in conferences and events that are presently impossible because of Sheba's insatiable demands. If, as some of the Ancient Egyptians thought, when we die we go to a heaven of cats, Johan will have the keys to the Kingdom. I may not be allowed in.

Occasionally, Johan tells me that I should start 'winding down' and 'acting my age'. When I remind him of how easily I become bored, he suggests that I take a course in the smelling of roses. 'Bugger the roses', I say. But then he submits that I should be thinking more of him. This is probably a conversation common in the households of A-type personalities. So life marches on with each decade concluding more quickly than the last.

If only I could go back to the Botany lawn and look again at the old man of thirty, enjoying the sunshine. If only I could film that extraordinary moment when two young men walked past the El Alamein Fountain in Kings Cross and, finding no coffee shop open, repaired to the apartment in Kirribilli, never to be parted. If only AIDS had not come along, with its burdens and fearful challenges as such a terrifying ordeal for so many precious friends. If only we were still in Canberra, walking under a million stars in the clear night, contemplating the puzzles of justice that would arise on the morrow. If only the inexorable ticking of the clock could be stopped and the beauty of the present could be kept forever. If only I could learn to smell the roses.

BIBLIOGRAPHY

INTRODUCTION
Brown, A.J. *Michael Kirby: Paradoxes/principles*, Federation Press, Sydney, 2011.
Freckelton, Ian S.C. and Selby Hugh *Appealing to the Future: Michael Kirby and his legacy*, Lawbrook Co., Sydney, 2009
Kirby, Michael 'Fifty years after Wolfenden', *Meanjin*, No. 3, 2007

1. OF FRECKLES, CROWNS AND CANES
Based on an address to the New South Wales Primary Principals' Association annual conference, Sydney, 29 October 2010.

2. AFTER WOLFENDEN
Australian Human Rights and Equal Opportunity Commission, *Same-sex: Same entitlements*, National inquiry into discrimination against people in same-sex relationships: financial and work-related entitlements and benefits, HREOC, 2007
Blackstone, William *'Peccatum illud horrible, inter chrisianon non nominandum', Commentries on the Laws of England*
Christensen, Cornelia V., *Kinsey: a biography*, Indiana University Press, Bloomington, 1971

Crompton, L. *Homosexuality and Civilisation*, Harvard University Press, Cambridge, 2002

Croom v. Tasmania, (1997) 191 CLR 119

Eskridge, W.N. and Hunter, M.D., *Sexuality, Gender and the Law*, Foundation Press, New York, 1997

Grey, A. *Quest for Justice: Towards homosexual emancipation*, Sinclair-Stevenson, London, 1992

Kinsey, A. et al. *Sexual Behaviour in the Human Male*, Saunders, Philadelphia, 1948

—*Sexual Behaviour in the Human Female*, Saunders, Philadelphia, 1953

Lacey, Nicola *A Life of H.L.A. Hart: The nightmare and the noble dream*, Oxford University Press, Oxford, 2004. [Professor Hart became a strong public proponent of the Wolfenden reforms, relying on the principles in J.S. Mills, *On Liberty* (1859), Legal Classics, 1992]

Naz Foundation v. Delhi & Ors (2009) 4LRC s. 838, per A.P. Shah and Muralidhar J. Pomeroy, W.B. Dr Kinsey and the Institute for Sex Research, Nelson, London, 1972

Toonen v. Australia (1994), International Human Rights Reports, vol. 97, no. 3

4. JOHAN

Crowe v. Graham (1968) 121 CLR 375

Ex parte McKay; re Crowe (1967) 85 WN (pt 1) (NSW) 438 (CA)

Kanfer, S. *Groucho: The life and times of Julius Henry Marx*, Vintage Books, New York, 2001

Obscene and Indecent Publications Act 1981 (NSW) s. 15(d)

6. OUT OF AFRICA

Cameron, Edwin *Witness to Aids*, I.B. Tauris & Co., New York, 2005

7. THE SALVOS

Drawn from a speech given to the Salvation Army Australian Eastern Territory, the Sydney Citadel, 31 March 2007.

Salvation Army of Australia, 'Positional statement—human sexuality', www.salvationarmy.org.au

8. THE PRINCE

Forbes, Rosita *India of the Princes*, The Book Club, London, 1939

INDEX

Abbot, Tony 95
Actors' Studio, New York 51
AIDS xii, 34, 40, 115–47, 151,
    171–2, 189; see also HIV
Akinola, Archbishop 138
Anderson, Professor John 186
Anglicanism 2–3, 11, 138
Arbitration Commission 85
Arbor Day 11
Arrau, Claudio 28
The Australian 111
Australian Broadcasting
    Commission 85, 87

Banda, Dr Hastings 132
Barton, Edmund 19
Barwick, Chief Justice 68
Bassein 173–6
    Fort 173–4, 179–81
Bentham, Jeremy 27, 32
Bergson, Pierre 110

Berlin Blockade 15
Black, Sir Hermann 10–11
The Blacksmith 10
Blackstone, William
    Commentaries on the Laws of
        England 27
Boermeister, Mrs 77, 83–4
Bonhoeffer, Dietrich 45
Book of Common Prayer 11
Booth, William 149, 150
Boutros-Gahli, Boutros 120
Bradfield, Dr 19
Brando, Marlon 51
British Empire 3–4, 127, 168
Bush, George W. 61

Callea, Anthony 163
Cameron, Justice Edwin 116, 117,
    121, 130, 173
    Witness to AIDS 116

Catechism of the Roman Catholic Church 190
cats 79–80, 92, 191–2
Censor 67, 68
censorship 67
Chifley, Ben 15, 16
Chiluba, Frederick 121–2, 132
Chinese Revolution 11, 15
Chong, Bobby 8–9, 14
Clancy, Cardinal Edward 97
Communist Party of Australia 16
Concord 2, 4, 5, 14, 85, 149
Concord Repatriation General Hospital 7
Constitutional Conference of Malawi 132
Council of Catholic School Parents 111
Cranmer, Archbishop Thomas 11
Crimes Act 1900 (NSW) 38
criminal laws 37–8
Croome, Rodney 35–6, 106
Cyclone Tracy 152

De Weerd, James 49, 51, 54
Dean, James Byron xii, 43–62
Dean, Mildred (nee Wilson) 49
Dean, Winton 49, 51
Delaney, Colin 28, 45, 66, 67, 68, 74, 86
Delhi High Court 39
Dixon, Sir Owen x
Demo 72–3, 74, 83, 186–7, 188
Departmental Committee on Homosexual Offences and Prostitution 25–6; *see also* Wolfenden Report
Dunstan, Don 28

East of Eden 46–8, 50, 51, 55
education 1–22
  Catholic schools 99
  Leaving Certificate 47
  opportunity classes 13–18
  public schools 21
  selective schools 19
  writing 4–5, 7–8, 18–19
Einfeld, Marcus 153
Ellis, Havelock 32
English Reforming Act 33–4
Evans, Gareth 35
Evatt, Dr H.V. 'Bert' 15, 19

Fairmount 43–9, 51–2, 57–8, 61
  Fairmount Historical Museum 52–3, 55
  The Legend 57–9
family and friends 1, 5–6, 16, 20–1, 85, 87, 108
  Diana (sister) 1, 3
  Donald (brother) 1, 3, 48, 105
  Norma (grandmother) 20, 150
  parents 5–6, 8–9, 16, 20–1, 85, 191
Fanny Hill 67
Federal politics 15–16
Ferber, Edna 53
Fiji 83–4
Flynn, Christopher 96, 100
Forbes, Rosita
  India of the Princes 167
Formosa-Taiwan 11
Fort Street Boys' High School 18–20, 71, 96, 102
Fort Street Girls' High School 19
Freud, Sigmund 32

Gallipoli 88–9
Gallo, Robert 122

Gaudron, Justice Mary 106, 191
Gay and Lesbian Mardi Gras
    97–8, 110–11
Geary, Luke 153, 154–5,1 60
Giant 47, 53
Gleeson, Murray 186
Gohil Rajpu dynasty 169–72
Gould League 12
Government House, Canberra 88
Graham, Richard 67–70
Great Durbar 170
Great War 1914–18 17
Grimm's Fairy Tales 20
GRIND (Gay Related Immuno
    Deficiency) 120

Harris, Julie 51
Heffernan, Senator Bill 185
Heidegger, Martin 110
Henry VIII 27, 35
High Court 36, 68, 86, 106, 108,
    153, 191
Hildebrand, Sraffan 123
Hill, Graham 16
HIV xii, 34, 40, 115–47, 151,
    171–2; *see also* AIDS
    discrimination legislation 135–6
    early experiences in Australian
        legal system 133–4
    rights-based approach 128–9,
        139, 143
homosexuality 25–40, 45
    decriminalisation 26–36
    'don't ask, don't tell' 29, 61, 87
    equalities and inequalities
        89–91
    human rights and 32, 35, 36–9
    Kinsey study 29–31, 60
    oppression, continuing existence
        of 39–40

post-Wolfenden reforms xii, 33
pre-Wolfenden reforms 28–9,
    45–6
public acknowledgement 107–8
public attitudes 36–7, 86,
    110–12
religious views 96–8, 104–5,
    107–11, 121–2, 137, 138,
    151, 157–9, 162–3
same-sex marriages 89–91, 141
Tasmania 34 6
Honi Soit 67
Horler, Ken 68
Howard, John 89, 95
Human Rights (Sexual Conduct)
    Act 1994 36
Hunt, Terence 10, 20
Hyderabad 168
hymns 10, 150

India 39, 167–9
    penal code 171
    princely states 168–70
Indiana University 52, 59, 60
    OUT 60–2
International Covenant on Civil and
    Political Rights 1966 35
International Herald Tribune 172

Jefferts Schori, Archbishop
    Katharine 138
Jeffrey, General Michael 88

Kashmir 168
Kaunda, Kenneth 132
Kazan, Elia 46, 51
Kelly, Ned 12
kindergarten 1–3
King Emperor George V 170
King George VI 8, 20

Kings Cross 69
Kinsey, Alfred 29–33, 38, 39, 40, 60
Kinsey Institute 60
Kipling, Rudyard 22
Knowles, William Spotswood (maternal grandfather) 21
Krafft-Ebing, Richard 32

Lakshya Trust 172, 177, 178, 179
'Law and Hypocrisy' 25–6
Law Reform Commission 86
lawmaking principles 27–8
Lawyers Collective (Mumbai) 118
Lee, Kuan Yew 39
Lewanika, David 126
Loft Inn 44–5, 49, 59
Loften, Mrs 44–5, 52, 59
love and companionship 66–93, 181

McCain, John 46, 61
McLelland, Charles 102
Macquarie University 11, 16
Mabo xi
Mahler, Halfdan 120, 122
Malawi 132
Mann, Jonathan 120, 121, 122
Marx, Groucho 65
Mawson, Douglas 19
Menzies, Robert 15–16, 19
Merson, Professor Mike 120
The Mikado 16
Mill, John Stuart 27, 32
Montagnier, Luc 122
Montagu, Edward 26
Moonlight, Captain 12
Movement for the Ordination of Women 106
MSMs 177–8

Mumbai 118, 171, 172, 173
Mwanawas, Levy Patrick 122

Nakajima, Hiroshi 120, 122
Nall, Adeline 50, 59
national anthems 126–7
Ndungeane, Archbishop Njongonkulu 138
Nehru, Jawajarlal 169
Netherlands, the 78–80
New South Wales Council for Civil Liberties 66–8
New Zealand 72
Nigeria 126–7, 132, 138
Nile, Reverend Fred 98
No. 96 188–9
Nuremburg Laws 37
Obscenity 67, 68

Oliver, Archbishop 145
Opera House 73

Pakistan 168
Panorama 80
Parliament House, Sydney 14
Pass Laws 37
Petersham Dance Hall 69–71, 73, 83
Piot, Peter 119–23
The Prayer 163–4
Prince Manvendra xiii, 170–83
Purple Onion 188

Quakers 49, 53, 62
Queen Elizabeth *I* 27
Queen Elizabeth II 27
Queen Empress Mary 170

Rajpipla 167, 169, 170, 173, 174, 178
Rebel Without A Cause 47, 57

Red Shield appeals 150
refugees 153
religious education 2–3
Rex, The 69–71, 73–4, 77, 83, 151, 187
Rietvelt, Bertha Aria 78
Riverview xiii, 96–112
    'Hot Potato Club' 95, 101–3, 112
    old boys 96–7
Roberts, Major Campbell 160–1, 163, 164
Robinson, Bishop V. 138
Rosenman, Leonard 47, 48
Royal Society of Ireland 20
Rudd, Kevin 89

St Andrew's Anglican Church 2, 11
Saint Francis Xavier 101–2
Saint Ignatius 101
St Ignatius College see Riverview
Sakala, Chief Justice Ernest 125, 128–9, 136–7, 142
Salvation Army xiii, 149–64
    social justice conference 153–7, 159–64
    statement on human sexuality 161–2
same-sex marriages 89–91, 141
School Magazine 7, 10
schools 1–22
    public 6, 21
    speaking at 96
Schubert, Franz 10
Second World War 5, 15, 78–9
Sen, Amartya 39
sexuality studies 29–30; see also homosexuality
Sidibé, Michel 123
Simpson, Jack 16

Singapore 39
Singh, Maharaja Vijay 170
Singhji, Maharaja Roghubir 170
social justice 103–4, 153
    churches 103–4
South Africa 115, 116, 141
Sozi, Dr Catherine 143, 144
Spencer, Brian 16
Spender, Bertram 19
Staples, Jim 68
Stevens, Bertram 19
Strathfield 2
Stone, Julius x
Strathfield North Public School 6–13, 105
    school song 12
Strong, Commissioner Les 155–6, 159–60, 164
Summer Hill Public School 13–18, 19
Sunday school 150
Sunday Telegraph 111
Sunday Times 26
Sydney Conservatorium of Music 12–13
Sydney Harbour Bridge 19, 72
Sydney Morning Herald 86, 111
Sydney University 11, 37, 67, 186
Symonds, James Addington 10

Tasmania 34–6
teachers 1–22, 109
    Casimir, Mr 9–10, 12
    Church, Mrs 1–3, 5
    Gibbons, Mr 17–18, 19
    Godwin, Mrs 7–8
    Gorringe, Mr 14–16
    Pontifex, Miss 4–5
    See, Mrs 5
    Tennant, Warren 17, 18

These Things Shall Be 10
Time magazine 61
Times of India 172
Toonen, Nicholas 35–6, 39
travel 83–5, 88–9, 118–19
Treatt, Vernon 38
Tutu, Bishop Desmond 39, 138

UNAIDS 118, 119, 123, 137
United Nations 15
  Human Rights Committee 35
Universal Declaration of Human
  Rights xiv, 15
University of Reading 25

van Vloten, Johan Anton xii,
  73–93, 141, 173, 182, 185–92
  and cats 79–80, 92, 191–2
van Vloten, Willem Nicholaas 78
Victoria Falls 118–19
Vietnam War 71
  conscientious objectors 67
von Ribbentrop, Joachim 76, 77,
  88

Wells, Dr Herman 60
Wesley, Charles 10, 149
Wesley, John 149

'White Australia' xi, 8, 11
Who's Who in Australia 185
Wik Peoples xi
Williams, David 188
Winslow, Marcus 49, 56
Winslow, Marcus Jr 50, 53–7
Winslow, Ortense 49, 50, 56
Wolfenden, Lord John 25, 32–3,
  38
Wolfenden Report 25–8, 32–4, 39,
  40
World Health Organization
  (WHO) 120,1 22
The World We Live In 10–11

youth suicide 98–9, 111

Zambia 121–47
  Bill of Rights 135
  HIV/AIDS statistics 116,
    129–30, 143
  religious influences 137
ZARAN (Zambian AIDSLaw
  Research Advocacy Network)
  115–47
Zeigler, Phil 52–9
Zimbabwe 39, 118